Just Enough
ENGLISH
GRAMMAR
Illustrated

Gabriele Stobbe

New   ico City
                                       nto

Library of Congress Cataloging-in-Publication Data

Stobbe, Gabriele
    Just enough English grammar illustrated / Gabriele Stobbe.
       p. cm. — (Just enough)
    ISBN 0-07-149232-1 (alk. paper)
    1. English language—Grammar.   I. Title.

  PE1112.S76   2007
  428.2—dc22   2007009870

To my son, Alexis George Stobbe,
whose support and unshakeable belief in my talents
assisted me in realizing my vision

The author also thanks Meaghan McLean (www.subscriptionart.com) for designing
the wonderful graphic illustrations that bring the book to life; Kimberly Werner
(www.DesignInterventionPA.com) for adding her artistic touch to the project; Beulah Hager
for proofreading the manuscript; Perry Meyer and Anna South for assistance with the
English text; and Cynthia Lennox, ESL professor at Duquesne University, for her suggestions
and feedback.

1 2 3 4 5 6 7 8 9 0   CTPS/CTPS 0 9 8 7

ISBN 978-0-07-149232-4
MHID   0-07-149232-1

Also available this series: Just Enough Spanish Grammar Illustrated

McGraw-Hill books are available at special quantity discounts to use as premiums and
sales promotions, or for use in corporate training programs. For more information, please
write to the Director of Special Sales, Professional Publishing, McGraw-Hill, Two Penn
Plaza, New York, NY 10121-2298. Or contact your local bookstore.

This book is printed on acid-free paper.

CONTENTS

INTRODUCTION

What This Book Contains

■ *Just Enough English Grammar Illustrated* requires no formal exposure to English grammar. The book is designed to give learners of English a basic grammar foundation. It may serve other students as a reference or review tool.

■ This book takes a practical approach. It does not focus on rules and definitions. Instead, it studies how words work and what they do in sentences.

■ The material is presented in an easy, step-by-step format. As the learner moves through the book, he or she will gain an understanding of the basic principles of the English language. These principles are laid out simply but thoroughly, and each new principle builds on what the student learned earlier in the book.

■ Real-life scenarios use interesting characters and engaging, simple vocabulary. Basic English structures presented in visually engaging graphics bring grammar alive and therefore increase the student's desire to learn grammar.

■ Carefully designed graphic illustrations translate grammatical concepts into visual images. Each topic or grammar concept is clearly explained with relevant graphic illustrations. They make comprehension possible without wordy explanations.

■ Graphic organizers and Venn diagrams clarify concepts and help the reader review. They stimulate creative and logical thought processes, and also help the student to evaluate and categorize language structures.

■ Review Exercises and the Answer Key provide the learner with the opportunity to test his or her skills.

■ This book offers choices. It takes into account the different ways in which students learn and, accordingly, provides a variety of learning tools. From real-life scenarios to illustrations and graphic organizers, there is something for everyone.

Organization of Chapters

Your Framework

The eight chapters of this book are organized around the eight parts of speech. It is important to become familiar with the name of each part of speech and to expand your knowledge about each one. The parts of speech will become the overall framework of your English language knowledge. It is to this framework that you will add important information necessary to build your basic grammar foundation.

The following strategies were designed to show you how these eight parts of speech can help you to build your foundation.

Your Strategies: Words are Tools for Communication

Strategy #1: How to Use Your Tools

Becoming familiar with your tools is the first strategy. Words are tools for communication. The vocabulary words used in this book were chosen because of their applicability to real-life scenarios. Your tools—a set of illustrated vocabulary words—are at the end of this Introduction. The players represented throughout the book are everyday people. They add spark and a new, refreshing approach to what is usually dry material. The illustrations of all key players are followed by brief biographies with interesting details about the lives of the main personalities.

Strategy #2: Basic Language Concept Number One: Form of the Eight Parts of Speech

Communication generally means putting words together to express your thoughts in context. Before you can put words together effectively, you must comprehend basic language concepts. This book emphasizes an understanding of key grammatical concepts over the memorization of individual words.

Most of the chapters in this book are divided into two parts. Typically, the part of speech that is the focus of the chapter is first discussed in terms of its *form*—the qualities that it has in common with other parts of speech. Then the *use* of each part of speech is considered.

What Information Do All of These Parts of Speech Give?

In this book, you will learn about three important concepts: number, gender, and grammar person. Part One of several of the chapters will show how these three concepts are expressed in the different parts of speech.

Strategy #3: Basic Language Concept Number Two: Use of the Eight Parts of Speech

What Jobs Can All of These Parts of Speech Do?

Part Two will build on what you learn in Part One. In many chapters, Part Two explains the jobs that different parts of speech perform in a sentence, as well as the relationships between different words within a sentence. A thorough understanding of the concepts covered in Part One will make Part Two seem much easier!

Your Tools: English Vocabulary Words

bikini	locker room	towel	life preserver
beach ball	suntan lotion	sunglasses	pool
flippers	umbrella	bathing suit	lifeguard chair
Mexican hat	air mattress	diving board	whistle
pool ladder	hamburger	hot dog	goggles

Your Players: Family and Friends

The Miller Family

Mr. Miller	Mrs. Miller	Anna Miller	Andy Miller
father	**mother**	**daughter**	**son**

the parents

Anna	Andy
sister	**brother**

Lakeside Pool Friends

Ben	Jake	Susan	Maria	Anna
the boy	**the boy**	**the girl**	**the girl**	**the girl**

the boys   the girls

Kelly	Andy	Charles Smith	Mrs. Miller
the young girl	**the young boy**	**the man**	**the woman**

the children   the pool manager   the teacher

MEET THE PLAYERS

Susan

Susan lives in Miami, Florida. She is 16 years old. Susan is the lifeguard at Lakewood Pool. She is also on the swim team. Susan always wears her lucky red swim cap to swim meets. She dates Ben. Susan has a little brother named Tim. Tim likes to cheer for Susan at swim meets. She also has a cat named Snowball. Susan and her best friend, Anna, enjoy shopping, and they often babysit for their neighbor Kelly.

Ben

Ben moved to Miami three years ago. He is 17 years old. Ben has an older sister named Claire. He also has a puppy named Shadow. He is good friends with Charles Smith, the pool manager. He joined the swim team two years ago. Ben joined because he liked Susan, but now he is a very serious swimmer. He is always competing with Jake. Ben has trouble with grammar at school. He wants to study grammar this summer. Ben likes to surf and go bowling when he is not at the pool.

Maria

Maria is an exchange student. She is from Mexico. She misses her family. Maria is 17 years old. Spanish is her native language. She hopes that her English will improve. Maria lives with Anna and her family. She is a very good swimmer, but she is not on the swim team. She enjoys going to the pool with Anna. This summer, she wants to learn more about American holidays and customs.

Anna

Anna moved to Miami six months ago. She is from Seattle. She is 16 years old. Anna works at the Lakewood Pool concession stand. Anna is best friends with Susan and is dating Jake. She has a brother named Andy. Her parents, Mr. and Mrs. Miller, volunteer at the pool often. Anna worries that Jake and Ben are too competitive. She hopes that the swim meet will not hurt her friendship with Susan. Anna enjoys going to the beach and baking brownies.

Jake

Jake is Ben's rival. He is 18 years old. All of the girls think he is cute. He dates Anna. Jake likes to show off and do cannonballs into the pool. Jake has two younger brothers, Frank and Ryan. He wants to swim in the Olympics. Jake spends most of his time at Lakewood Pool. He really wants to beat Ben in the next swim meet. Jake hopes that he will get to spend time with Anna this summer.

CHAPTER 1

NOUNS

Nouns Adjectives Pronouns Verbs Adverbs Prepositions Conjunctions Interjections

1.1 Part One and Part Two Overview

In this first chapter, an important basic concept, the noun, is introduced. Nouns are a powerful part of speech. Here is a summary of the material about the form and uses of nouns covered in this chapter.

Part One: Form of English Nouns
What Information Do Nouns Give?

Types of Nouns
Number of Nouns
Noun Suffixes
Gender of Nouns
Articles

Part Two: Uses of English Nouns
What Jobs Can Nouns Do?

Nouns as Subjects
Nouns as Subject Complements
Possessive Nouns
Nouns as Direct Objects
Nouns as Objects of Prepositions

PART ONE: FORM OF ENGLISH NOUNS
What Information Do Nouns Give?

> **Form** refers to the qualities and characteristics
> that nouns have in common.

Let's start with the different types of nouns.

1.2 Types of Nouns

> A **noun** is a word used to name a person,
> place, thing, or idea.

A *noun* is one of the most important words you use when speaking and writing. A noun names a person, place, or thing; a quality, idea, or action.

We can classify or group nouns into the following categories: proper, common, concrete, abstract, collective, and compound nouns. The following chart explains these classifications.

Types of Nouns

Susan	**Proper**	Proper nouns label specific people, places, or things. The first letter must be capitalized.
school	**Common**	Common nouns label general groups, places, people, or things.
hamburger	**Concrete**	Concrete nouns label things experienced through the senses of sight, hearing, taste, smell, and touch.
love	**Abstract**	Abstract nouns label things not knowable through the senses.
family	**Collective**	Collective nouns label groups as a unit.
suntan lotion	**Compound**	Compound nouns label a single concept composed of two or more words.

Note: A noun can belong to more than one group. For example, **suntan lotion** is both a common and a concrete noun, as well as a compound noun.

1.3 One or Many: Singular and Plural Nouns

Nouns carry information about *number*. When a word refers to one person or thing, it is singular in number. When it refers to more than one of the same type of thing, it is plural in number.

One   More Than One

Singular   Plural

The *number* of a noun is indicated by its ending. The final letters of a noun determine how its plural is formed.

The following examples illustrate how to change from the singular form of a noun to the plural form of a noun.

The plural of most nouns is formed by adding **-s**.

ball   balls

For nouns ending in **s**, **x**, **z**, **sh**, and **ch**, add **-es**.

watch   watch**es**

Nouns ending in **f** or **fe** form their plurals by changing the **f** or **fe** to **v** and adding **-es**.

wife   wi**ves**

Nouns ending in **y** form their plurals by changing the **y** to **i** and adding **-es**.

family   famil**ies**

Take a look at other noun endings to discover other irregular noun plurals.

1.4 A Closer Look at Noun Endings: Common Noun Suffixes

The main part of a word is called the *root*. Suffixes are added to the end of the root. A suffix consists of one or more letters or syllables added to the end of a root to change its meaning.

Adding **-er** indicates the person who is carrying out an action.

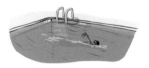

Example: A person who swims is a swimm**er**.

Note: Because of spelling rules, the **-m-** is doubled.

Adding **-ance** indicates the fact or state of carrying out an action.

Example: Someone who performs gives a perform**ance**.

Adding **-ness** indicates a quality or state of being.

Example: The state of being happy is happi**ness**.

Note: Because of spelling rules, the **-y** changes to **-i-**.

Adding **-ity** indicates an action or state of affairs that is abstract.

Example: Something that is possible
is a possibi**lity**.

Note: Because of spelling rules, the **-e-** is dropped.

Recognizing these suffixes can help you to identify nouns.
The ability to distinguish nouns from other words is very useful.

1.5 The Biological Nature: Masculine, Feminine, and Neuter Nouns

English nouns do not have gender. That is, they are not
inherently masculine or feminine. However, they may refer
to male or female people or animals. When things have no clear
gender, they are often said to be inanimate objects or things,
and they are thought of as being neuter.

Masculine Nouns

Nouns that refer to male people or animals
are *masculine nouns.*

Examples:
Mr. Miller, man, father, actor, bull

Feminine Nouns

Nouns that refer to female people or animals
are *feminine nouns.*

Examples:
Mrs. Miller, woman, mother, actress, cow

Neuter Nouns

Nouns that denote things of neither gender
are *neuter nouns.*

Examples:
locker, ball, towel, lotion

Nouns often come in the company of other words. It is important to learn about these little words, since they signal that a noun follows, and this could assist you in identifying nouns more easily.

1.6 In the Company of a Noun: Articles

Nouns are often accompanied by *articles*, also commonly called *noun namers*. These are placed before a noun.

Articles

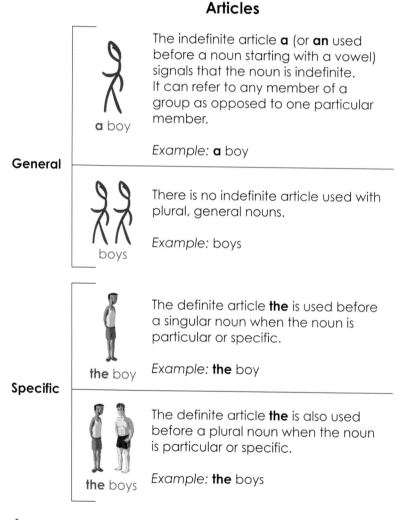

General

a boy

The indefinite article **a** (or **an** used before a noun starting with a vowel) signals that the noun is indefinite. It can refer to any member of a group as opposed to one particular member.

Example: **a** boy

boys

There is no indefinite article used with plural, general nouns.

Example: boys

Specific

the boy

The definite article **the** is used before a singular noun when the noun is particular or specific.

Example: **the** boy

the boys

The definite article **the** is also used before a plural noun when the noun is particular or specific.

Example: **the** boys

! *Hint:* **A** *is used before words beginning with a consonant;* **an** *is used before words beginning with a vowel.*

Noun Starting with a Consonant   **Noun Starting with a Vowel**

Example: **a** beach towel   *Example:* **an** air mattress

Part One looked at the form of nouns. Many concepts introduced in this section will appear again later in this book. Next, let's take a closer look at what nouns can do.

PART TWO: USES OF ENGLISH NOUNS
What Jobs Can Nouns Do?

1.7 From Form to Use of Nouns

Nouns have jobs to do.

When you express a thought or idea in a sentence, you place words into what is called *context*. Nouns are assigned different roles or jobs to do when they are used in sentences. Here is an example to illustrate use and context.

The context for all these things is their use in water.

What is wrong with this picture? If Maria wants to wear her bathing suit, she needs a pool, a lake, or the sea to put it to use. Here in the desert, she is in the wrong environment to wear a bathing suit: It is not the right context.

Similarly, words have jobs to do for which they are suited. When you put a sentence together that is grammatically correct, you give each part the right job to do.

1.8 When Nouns Become Subjects

Nouns have specific jobs to do when placed within a sentence. These jobs are labeled as subjects, subject complements, possessive nouns, or objects. Let's look at each.

The first, and most important, job that nouns can do in a sentence is to act as a *subject*.

The chart below shows how nouns become subjects. They are still nouns, but they are now called subjects in the form of a noun. They are the focus of the sentence, and their job is to carry out the action described by the verb.

> **A noun that names the person(s) or thing(s) about which a statement is to be made is labeled the *subject*.**

Nouns as Subjects

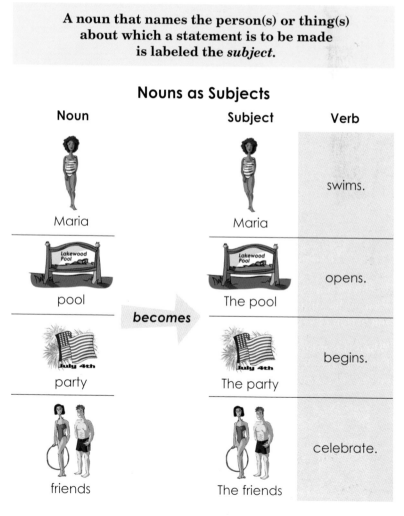

Noun	Subject	Verb
Maria	Maria	swims.
pool	The pool	opens.
party	The party	begins.
friends	The friends	celebrate.

becomes

Any type of noun can become a subject.

Nouns referring to people often act as subjects and are easily recognized:

Proper Nouns	Common Nouns
Ben Maria Mr. and Mrs. Miller	man swimmer girl

Nouns referring to inanimate objects can also be used as subjects:

chair   swimsuit   suntan lotion   school

To find the subject of a sentence, use a question word. When the subject is a person, use the question word **Who**: For example, for the sentence **Ben swims**, ask **Who** swims? The answer is **Ben**.

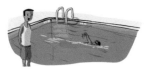

Example: Ben swims.
Who swims? **Ben** swims.

In the example above, the statement is about Ben. The noun **Ben** is the subject of the sentence **Ben swims**. Ben performs the action of swimming. The verb **swims** tells what Ben does.

When the subject is not a person, use the question word **What**: For example, for the sentence **The pool opens**, ask **What** opens? The answer is **The pool**.

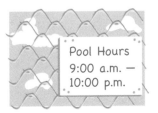

Pool Hours
9:00 a.m. —
10:00 p.m.

Example: The pool opens.
What opens? **The pool** opens.

10

In this example, the noun **pool** is the thing about which something is said. The verb **opens** tells what is happening to the subject.

Ben swims and **The pool opens** are two examples illustrating the smallest type of sentence: a subject and a verb. Both sentences make a statement with the subject followed by the verb.

Finding and recognizing the subject in a sentence is an essential skill to develop. More details about sentence structure follow as we explain more about the different uses of nouns.

Here is another important rule to remember:

> **A sentence must have both a subject and a verb, and it must express a complete thought.**

1.9 Simple and Compound Subjects

A sentence may have two or more nouns used as subjects and two or more verbs.

Complete Sentence

Example: **Ben** swims.

Simple Subject   Verb

In the sentence **Ben swims**, Ben performs the action. **Ben** is a singular noun. When just one noun is used as the subject, we call the subject a *simple subject*. The noun can be either singular or plural.

> **When a sentence has two or more nouns used as subjects that are joined by "and," it has a *compound subject*.**

Example: **Hamburgers and hot dogs** are popular.

Compound Subject

11

The words **hamburgers and hot dogs** are the compound subject in this sentence. A compound subject is composed of two or more nouns used as subjects. These nouns can be either singular or plural. They represent the things about which something is being said.

In the next section, you will learn how nouns can express a different concept when they are in the company of another noun.

1.10 When One Noun Is Not Enough: Subject Complements

Example:
The hamburger is the winner.

／ ＼

Subject   *Subject Complement*

Fred found out what customers like best!

In this example, the noun **hamburger** is the subject. **The winner**, another noun, is the complement that describes or renames the hamburger. It is called a *subject complement* because it gives more details about the subject **hamburger**.

> **A *subject complement*
> describes or renames the subject.**

Example:

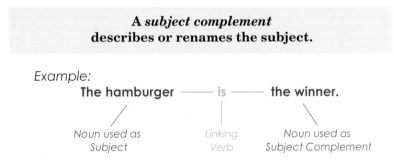

The hamburger ——— is ——— **the winner.**

／ | ＼

Noun used as Subject   *Linking Verb*   *Noun used as Subject Complement*

The verb **is** links **hamburger** to **winner**. For that reason, it is called a *linking verb*. Linking verbs help to make a statement not by expressing an action, but by serving as a link between the subject and the subject complement.

Am, **are**, **is**, **was**, and **were** are all forms of the most commonly used linking verb **to be**.

> **Subject complements are placed *after* a linking verb.**

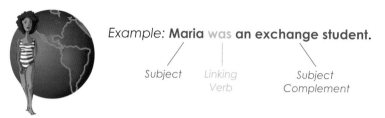

Example: **Maria** was **an exchange student.**

Subject   Linking   Subject
          Verb   Complement

In this example, the name **Maria** is the subject. The linking verb **was** is followed by the phrase **an exchange student**, which renames or describes the subject **Maria**. That makes the noun **exchange student** the subject complement.

In your mind, replace the linking verb with an equals sign to remember that both nouns are of equal value. In the first example, **hamburger = winner**, and in the second, **Maria = exchange student**. Any form of **to be**, when it acts as a linking verb, can be represented by an equals sign.

You will learn more about linking verbs in Chapter 4.

1.11 Possessive Nouns: Showing Relationship or Ownership

Now you will learn how to change the form of a noun to indicate a close relationship (often ownership) to another noun.

> **To show relationship or ownership of a noun, add an apostrophe, either with or without the letter *s*.**

If the singular form of the noun *doesn't end in* **s**, add an apostrophe followed by the letter **s** (**'s**).

Example with Relationship:

the pool   ➜   diving board

the pool**'s** diving board

Singular Noun

*what is
being related to*

Possessive Noun

13

the chil**d's** ball

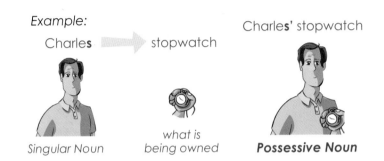

the chil**d** ⟶ ball

Singular Noun   *what is being owned*   **Possessive Noun**

If the singular form of the noun *does end in* **s**, add only the apostrophe (**'**).

Example:

Charle**s** ⟶ stopwatch

Charle**s'** stopwatch

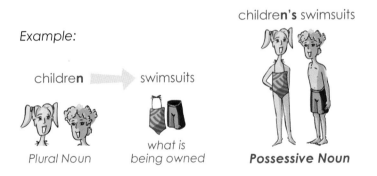

Singular Noun   *what is being owned*   **Possessive Noun**

You can apply the same rule to plural possessive nouns.
If the plural form of the noun *doesn't end in* **s**, add an apostrophe followed by the letter **s** (**'s**).

childre**n's** swimsuits

Example:

childre**n** ⟶ swimsuits

Plural Noun   *what is being owned*   **Possessive Noun**

If the plural form of the noun *does end in* **s**, add only the apostrophe (**'**), for example, **the kids' swimsuits**.

Possessive nouns indicate the relationship between an owner and something that is being owned.

A possessive noun always uses an apostrophe.

14

When showing possession, you can choose between two options to indicate that relationship. We just explained the use of an apostrophe for possessive nouns. We'll now explain how to use the "of" phrase.

Example:
the diving board of the pool

Here is a simple way to convert the possessive noun to an "of" phrase: Use **of** instead of the apostrophe, and switch the order of the nouns.

Example:
the pool's diving board = the diving board of the pool

Hint: Be sure you understand the use of an apostrophe to show ownership. Apostrophes are also used for contractions, which are shortened forms of certain words. For example, **it's** = **it is**, **you've** = **you have**. *More details about contractions follow in Chapter 4, Verbs.*

An important rule to remember:

A possessive noun formed with an apostrophe always relates to another noun that indicates what is being owned.

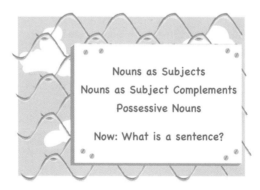

Nouns as Subjects
Nouns as Subject Complements
Possessive Nouns

Now: What is a sentence?

So far, we've learned about nouns as subjects, nouns as subject complements, and possessive nouns. Let's pause here and take a look at how to form sentences.

15

1.12 What Is a Sentence? Building Blocks and Units

Building blocks used together form a unit.

You have learned that a noun becomes the subject of a sentence when it is connected to a verb as the performer of that action. In a sentence, the subject and the verb need each other in order to make sense. Let's replace the word "sentence" with the term "unit." *Units* are composed of different parts that we will call *building blocks*. They must be placed in such a way that the unit is complete and makes sense.

Example:

Jake   Jake swims.

Proper Noun   Subject Noun   Verb

Subject and Verb form a Unit.

Jake, the subject, is a building block. The noun **Jake** will not be a subject if you separate it from the verb. In order to label **Jake** as the subject, he needs to perform an action, in this case, swimming. When you put these two parts—**Jake** (subject) and **swims** (verb)—together, you form the simplest possible unit.

Use a period to indicate that your *sentence* or *unit* is complete:

Jake swims.

You have also learned that a noun can be used as a subject complement when it is connected to the subject through a linking verb. Here we have the building blocks of a subject (**hamburger**) and a subject complement (**winner**) that must be connected by a linking verb (**is**) to be complete and make sense. Thus, together they form a unit.

Example:

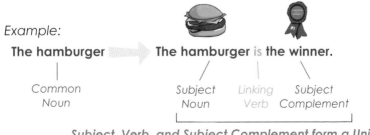

The hamburger   The hamburger is the winner.

Common   Subject   Linking   Subject
Noun   Noun   Verb   Complement

Subject, Verb, and Subject Complement form a Unit.

16

Use a period to indicate that your sentence or unit is complete:

The hamburger is the winner.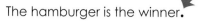

Possessive nouns also show a connection between two nouns. Let's take a look at the noun **Anna** and the noun **hula hoop**.

Example:

Anna's hula hoop — Can you add a period here?
/
Possessive Noun

If you add a period, you would indicate that the sentence is complete—that someone or something is doing an action. That someone or something would be the subject that is performing the action of a verb. Is Anna performing an action? No, Anna is not connected to a verb. The verb is missing. The possessive noun **Anna's** only indicates a relationship between the two nouns. As shown by the apostrophe, the hula hoop belongs to Anna.

Example:

Building Block
Anna's hula hoop
/
Possessive Noun

Anna's hula hoop represents a building block. It is not a unit, because a unit must contain a subject and a verb, and this has no verb. However, you can use this possessive noun to create a unit.

Example:

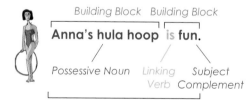

Building Block   Building Block
Anna's hula hoop is fun.
/   /   \
Possessive Noun Linking   Subject
              Verb   Complement

Subject, Verb, and Subject Complement form a Unit.

Expanding units to include other ideas is the next step to take. And remember that it's easier to enlarge units when you know where to find the subject.

*We will now take a big step by learning what **objects** can do.*

1.13 When Verbs Expand to Include Objects: Direct Objects

Look at the following example to see how adding another noun to a sentence expresses a new concept.

Example:

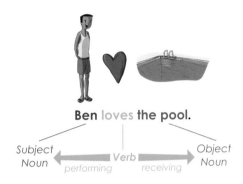

Ben loves **the pool.**

This sentence includes two nouns. **Ben,** a proper noun, performs the action of loving. The basic unit of subject and verb is **Ben loves.** The verb is then extended by adding another noun, **the pool.** It is placed after the verb and directly receives the action expressed by the verb **loves.**

> **The *direct object* is a word or group of words that directly receives the action expressed by the verb.**

Verbs that can take direct objects are called *action verbs.* Here are four action verbs.

write   eat   love   swim

> **Direct objects need action verbs.**

Action verbs are verbs that express something that we do. Here are four sentences with direct objects. Each sentence is divided into two parts to illustrate the verb-object connection first, and then the subject-verb connection.

18

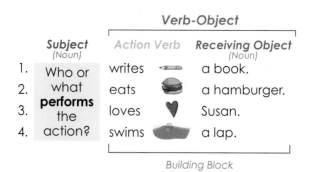

Verb-Object

	Subject *(Noun)*	Action Verb		Receiving Object *(Noun)*
1.	Who or what **performs** the action?	writes		a book.
2.		eats		a hamburger.
3.		loves		Susan.
4.		swims		a lap.

Building Block

In each of the four examples, action verbs and their direct objects are shown. What is missing? Yes, you need a person or thing performing the action.

Subject-Verb

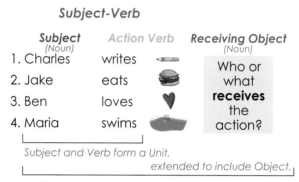

	Subject *(Noun)*	Action Verb		Receiving Object *(Noun)*
1.	Charles	writes		Who or what **receives** the action?
2.	Jake	eats		
3.	Ben	loves		
4.	Maria	swims		

Subject and Verb form a Unit,
extended to include Object.

Charles writes, **Jake eats**, **Ben loves**, and **Maria swims** are four sentences that are complete with a subject and a verb. The sentences could end there, and you could add a period after each one. However, they were extended to include **writes a book**, **eats a hamburger**, **loves Susan**, and **swims a lap**. These groups of words are building blocks. They cannot stand alone.

Let's join the two parts together. If you start with the verb in the center, you can think of the verb as reaching out to both sides. One side of the verb reaches for the subject, the other side reaches for the object.

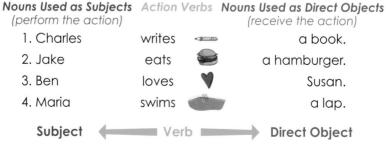

Nouns Used as Subjects *(perform the action)*	Action Verbs		Nouns Used as Direct Objects *(receive the action)*
1. Charles	writes		a book.
2. Jake	eats		a hamburger.
3. Ben	loves		Susan.
4. Maria	swims		a lap.

Subject ⟵ **Verb** ⟶ **Direct Object**

It is important to recognize how the different parts relate to each other. Take the example of the Miller family. A mother and father—Mr. and Mrs. Miller—are the core of a family. Children and other members are additions to that family. When they are together, they form a unit: the Miller family.

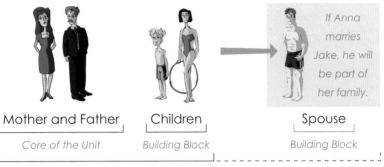

Mother and Father	Children	Spouse
Core of the Unit	Building Block	Building Block

If Anna marries Jake, he will be part of her family.

Together, they form the Miller family.

Jake, still part of his own family, could become an additional member of the Miller family.

Similarly, a sentence has a subject and verb that form a core unit. The direct object you add represents a building block that depends on the core unit to make complete sense.

The following chart illustrates the different roles nouns assume in sentences. The nouns **book**, **hamburger**, **Susan**, and **lap** are used first as objects, and then as subjects.

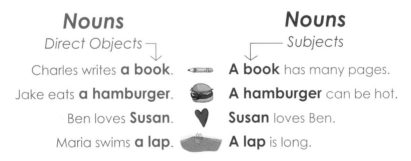

Nouns
Direct Objects

Charles writes **a book**.

Jake eats **a hamburger**.

Ben loves **Susan**.

Maria swims **a lap**.

Nouns
Subjects

A book has many pages.

A hamburger can be hot.

Susan loves Ben.

A lap is long.

Sometimes it is hard to recognize the subjects or objects of a sentence. Use question words to assist you with this process.

Question words can refer to persons or things. They can help you identify the subject or the object. The following explanations will give you a short overview. More details follow later in this book.

Question Words to Identify a Subject

Who

Identify subjects that are people using the question word **Who**:

To identify who is performing the action, the question word is placed **before** the verb.

Examples: Ben loves Susan.   Maria swims a lap.
              Who loves Susan?   **Who** swims a lap?
              /   \\   /   \\
      Question Word Verb   *Question Word Verb*

What

Identify subjects that are inanimate things with the question word **What**:

The question word that identifies the subject is placed **before** the verb.

Examples: The pool opens.   The towel is big.
            What opens?   **What** is big?
             /   \\   / \\
     Question Word Verb   *Question Word Verb*

Question Words to Identify a Direct Object

Direct objects, just like subjects, can be either people or things. Notice the question words used to identify the direct objects.

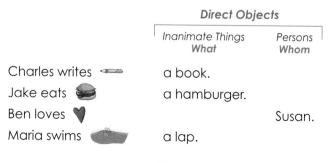

	Direct Objects	
	Inanimate Things *What*	*Persons* *Whom*
Charles writes	a book.	
Jake eats	a hamburger.	
Ben loves		Susan.
Maria swims	a lap.	

21

Identify people as direct objects using the question word **Whom**:

To identify who is receiving the action, place the question word *after* the verb.

Example: Ben loves Susan.
    Ben **loves whom**?

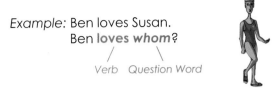

Verb Question Word

Identify inanimate things as direct objects with the question word **What**:

To identify what is receiving the action, place the question word *after* the verb.

Example: Charles writes a book.
    Charles **writes what**?

Verb Question Word

This section explained nouns used as direct objects. The next section introduces nouns as the object of a preposition.

1.14 Another Type of Object: Objects of Prepositions

There are two different types of objects. The object described above receives the action of the verb directly. It is called the *direct object*. The other object works together with a *preposition*. Prepositions and prepositional phrases are introduced in Chapter 6. At this point, we will just help you understand how nouns used as objects of a preposition are employed in a sentence.

Example: **around the pool**

Preposition Object of Preposition

In the example above, **around the pool** is a prepositional phrase that includes the preposition **around** and the noun **pool** as the object of the preposition.

Example: **under** the lifeguard chair

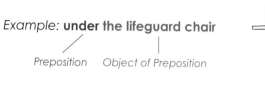

Preposition   Object of Preposition

In this example, **under the lifeguard chair**, the preposition **under** takes the noun **lifeguard chair** as the object of the preposition.

The combination of a preposition and an object is called a *prepositional phrase*. Phrases by themselves are only fragments, or building blocks. They must be combined with other parts to form a complete sentence or unit.

Let's connect the phrase **around the pool** with the noun **Susan** and the verb **walks** to form a complete sentence. When we add **Susan** as the subject, we must also include the verb, since **Susan**, as the subject, performs the action of the verb.

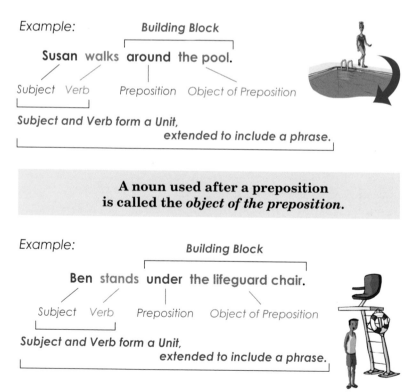

Example:

Building Block

Susan walks around the pool.

Subject   Verb   Preposition   Object of Preposition

Subject and Verb form a Unit,
extended to include a phrase.

> **A noun used after a preposition
> is called the *object of the preposition*.**

Example:

Building Block

Ben stands under the lifeguard chair.

Subject   Verb   Preposition   Object of Preposition

Subject and Verb form a Unit,
extended to include a phrase.

1.15 Overview of Uses of Nouns

Congratulations! You now have learned about the many jobs nouns can do. Nouns play an important part when building your understanding of the English language. We conclude this chapter with a Venn diagram that summarizes how the noun **trophy** can be used when forming sentences.

This diagram shows you that no matter what job nouns are doing, they remain nouns.

Venn Diagram

The next summary illustrates the jobs nouns can do by using the noun **Maria**.

Maria as Subject: **Maria** swims.

Maria as Subject Complement: The student is **Maria.**

Maria as Possessive Noun: **Maria's** bathing suit

Maria as Direct Object: Anna loves **Maria.**

Maria as Object of the Preposition *for*: The gift is for **Maria.**

1.16 Review Exercises

A Determine whether or not the word in red type is a noun.
If it is a noun, write **Y** for yes; if it is not a noun, write **N** for no.

1. Susan eats lunch. _____
2. The rabbit jumps. _____
3. Jake wants to run. _____
4. They live in Florida. _____
5. He reads a book. _____
6. She walks the dog. _____
7. Is the tree tall? _____
8. He writes a letter. _____
9. The glass is not full. _____
10. Ben cuts an apple. _____

B Write the plural form of each singular noun.
Example: child → children

1. ring _____
2. leaf _____
3. beach _____
4. cloud _____
5. berry _____
6. life _____
7. bird _____
8. patch _____
9. nail _____
10. sky _____

C Complete each sentence with either **a** or **an**.

1. He rides ____ blue bike.
2. Maria sees ____ airplane.
3. The dog has ____ bone.
4. Ben throws ____ ball.
5. She uses ____ umbrella.

D Underline the subject of each sentence. Circle the verb.

1. He runs.
2. Anna swims.
3. The father drives.
4. They sit.
5. The cat jumps.

E Write the possessive form of each noun.
Example: boy → boy's

1. trees   _____
2. bike   _____
3. Chris   _____
4. building   _____
5. cars   _____

F Underline the subject of each sentence. Circle its complement.

1. Her house is big.
2. The dog is brown.
3. He is short.
4. His name is Andy.
5. Is the sky blue?

G Determine whether each statement is true or false. Write **T** for true or **F** for false.

1. The direct object receives the action of the verb. _____
2. English nouns have a specific gender. _____
3. A compound subject is composed of two or more nouns used as subjects. _____
4. A sentence must have a subject and a verb. _____
5. "A" and "an" are indefinite articles. _____

CHAPTER 2

ADJECTIVES

2.1 What Is an Adjective?

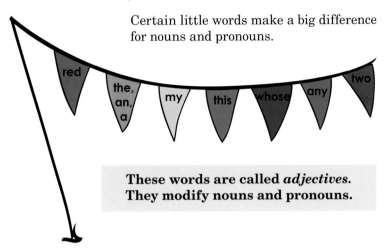

Certain little words make a big difference for nouns and pronouns.

**These words are called *adjectives*.
They modify nouns and pronouns.**

This chapter introduces two groups of adjectives: *descriptive adjectives* and *determiners* or *limiting adjectives*. In grammar, we say that an adjective modifies the meaning of a noun or pronoun.

Modifiers make clearer or limit the meaning of other words.

2.2 Descriptive Adjectives

***Descriptive adjectives* specify the shape, size, or color of the noun they modify.**

Descriptive adjectives are often called *common adjectives.* Like a common noun, they are ordinary, everyday adjectives. They describe a noun in a general way. Examples of common adjectives include **soft**, **blue**, **sunny**, **small**, and **wet**.

In general, common adjectives are placed before the noun they are describing, as the following examples illustrate.

Examples:

blue ball
/ \
Descriptive Adjective Noun

wet flippers
/ \
Descriptive Adjective Noun

An adjective can also come after the linking verb **to be** when the adjective describes the subject of a sentence. In this case, it is called a *predicate adjective*.

Example: The hamburger is **large**.
/ / \
Subject   Linking   Predicate
Verb   Adjective

In this example, the adjective **large** describes the subject **hamburger**. Calling it a **large hamburger** is the same as stating **The hamburger is large**.

Example: The flippers are **green**.
/ / \
Subject   Linking   Predicate
Verb   Adjective

In this example, the adjective **green** describes the subject **flippers**. Calling them **green flippers** is the same as stating **The flippers are green**.

> ***Predicate adjectives*** **are placed after the linking verb.**
> **They always expand on the subject.**

Descriptive adjectives can also be formed from a proper noun.

> **An adjective formed from a proper noun is called**
> **a *proper adjective*. It is always capitalized.**

Proper Noun	Proper Adjective		Example
Mexico	Mexican		Mexican student
America	American		American flag

Proper adjectives can be formed from the name of a particular person, place, thing, or idea.

2.3 Determiners or Limiting Adjectives

The second group of adjectives is called *determiners*. Since determiners limit your choices, they are also called *limiting adjectives*. A determiner is placed before the noun it modifies.

> **A *determiner* helps to identify a specific noun**
> **rather than describe it.**

Articles

> ***Articles* specify whether a noun is referred to in a general or specific way.**

The most frequently used adjectives are **a, an**, and **the**. These words are usually called *articles*.

There are two different types of articles: *indefinite articles* and *definite articles*.

Indefinite Articles

a boy **an** exchange student

A and **an** refer to one of a general group. Use **an** before a noun starting with a vowel. In the example **a boy**, we don't know which boy is being referred to.

Definite Articles

the friends

The indicates that the noun (either singular or plural) refers to someone or something in particular. In the example **the friends**, we are indicating this specific group of people.

Possessive Adjectives

> ***Possessive adjectives* are based on subject pronouns and show ownership or relationship.**

I, you, he, she, it, we, you, and **they** are called *personal pronouns*. In this term, the word *personal* relates to "persons." Possessive adjectives, as the following chart shows, are derived from these personal pronouns and express the idea of possession. With the exception of **it**, all of them relate to people.

Possessive Adjectives

Singular	① my	② your	③ his	her	its
Plural	① our	② your	③ their		

Examples:

The possessive adjective can express ownership or relationship. In English, the possessive adjectives **his** and **her** relate to the person who is the possessor. Look at the following examples:

his sister Anna
/ \
Masculine   Feminine
Possessive   Noun
Adjective

Masculine Possessive Adjective
+ Feminine Noun

her brother Andy
/ \
Feminine   Masculine
Possessive   Noun
Adjective

Feminine Possessive Adjective
+ Masculine Noun

In the first example, **his** modifies the noun **sister**. In the second example, **her** modifies the noun **brother**.

Demonstrative Adjectives

4

Demonstrative adjectives **point out persons or things. They can point to either singular or plural forms.**

this suntan lotion
/ \
Singular Form   Singular Noun
Demonstrative
Adjective

those flip-flops
/ \
Plural Form   Plural Noun
Demonstrative
Adjective

This and **that** are singular; **these** and **those** are plural. They are all *demonstrative adjectives* that point out specific nouns.

Interrogative Adjectives

5

Interrogative adjectives **are used to form questions. They single out the nouns they modify.**

The interrogative adjectives **which**, **what**, and **whose**, together with the nouns they modify, are commonly used to form questions.

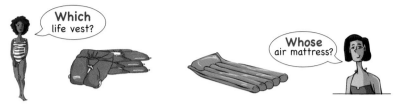

In the first example above, **which** modifies the noun **life vest**. In the second example, **whose** modifies the noun **air mattress** and is used to indicate ownership.

Indefinite Adjectives

> *Indefinite adjectives* indicate
> nonspecific persons or things.

6

Some, **each**, **any**, **many**, and **several** are examples of *indefinite adjectives*.

some girls

|

Indefinite *Adjective*

several lockers

|

Indefinite *Adjective*

In both of the examples above, we are not certain about the exact number of persons or things. As adjectives, **some** and **several** modify the nouns **girls** and **lockers**.

Numerical Adjectives

> *Numerical adjectives* indicate quantity by stating
> a fixed number of people or things.

7

one hot dog
/   \

Numerical Singular
Adjective Noun

two whistles
/   \

Numerical Plural
Adjective Noun

In the example **one hot dog, one** is the numerical adjective that indicates one in number. It is used with a singular noun. In the second example, the adjective **two** indicates two in number, and it must be used with a plural noun.

This concludes the section on determiners or limiting adjectives. Keep in mind the following rule:

Determiners indicate that a noun follows.

2.4 Suffixes and Origin of Adjectives

Many adjectives can be identified by their suffixes. Suffixes are attached to a root word to form the adjective. These adjectives originate from other types of words, such as nouns or verbs.

Some commonly used suffixes and their meanings follow.

Jake is a fear**less** swimmer.

less means *without*
fear is the root word

It was a wonder**ful** party.

ful means *full of*
wonder is the root word

The goggles are break**able**.

able means *capable of*
break is the root word

Review the comparative and superlative forms of adjectives in Chapter 5, Adverbs.

2.5 Overview of Adjectives

The following summary highlights the most important details about adjectives. Always begin by identifying the nouns first.

Summary of Adjectives

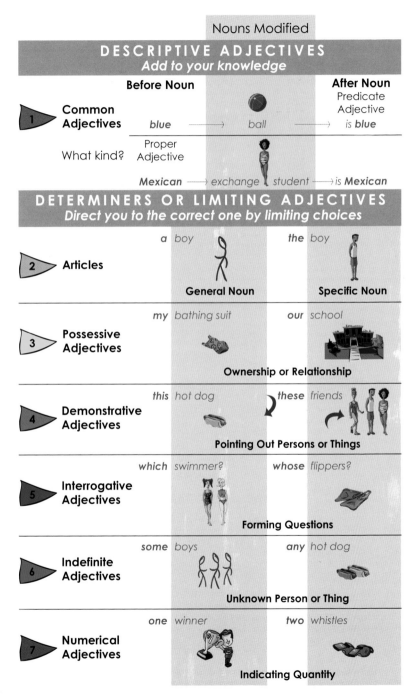

Nouns Modified

DESCRIPTIVE ADJECTIVES
Add to your knowledge

Before Noun   **After Noun**

1   Common Adjectives

Predicate Adjective

blue ⟶ ball ⟶ is blue

What kind?   Proper Adjective

Mexican ⟶ exchange ↓ student ⟶ is Mexican

DETERMINERS OR LIMITING ADJECTIVES
Direct you to the correct one by limiting choices

2   Articles

a boy   the boy

General Noun   Specific Noun

3   Possessive Adjectives

my bathing suit   our school

Ownership or Relationship

4   Demonstrative Adjectives

this hot dog   these friends

Pointing Out Persons or Things

5   Interrogative Adjectives

which swimmer?   whose flippers?

Forming Questions

6   Indefinite Adjectives

some boys   any hot dog

Unknown Person or Thing

7   Numerical Adjectives

one winner   two whistles

Indicating Quantity

2.6 Review Exercises

A Underline the descriptive adjective or adjectives in each sentence.

1. The music is loud.
2. She waves the American flag.
3. The brown horse jumps.
4. The small cup is full.
5. He has an orange balloon.
6. The tired girl sleeps.
7. The water is cold.
8. She plays a sad song.
9. The colorful painting is beautiful.

B Underline the article in each sentence. Decide whether it is definite or indefinite, and then write **D** for definite or **I** for indefinite.

1. She reads a book. _____
2. Does the cat purr? _____
3. He lives on an island. _____
4. A boy is yelling! _____
5. They go to the lake. _____

C Underline the limiting adjective or adjectives in each sentence.

1. His coat is black.
2. I have three brothers.
3. This is my house.
4. She swims every day!
5. We play at my house.
6. I want that one.
7. Susan is her friend.

CHAPTER 3

PRONOUNS

3.1 Part One and Part Two Overview

Pronouns are substitutes for nouns. The prefix "pro-" in the word *pronoun* means "for." The word *pronoun* simply means "for a noun" or "in place of a noun." Part One will take a closer look at the various forms pronouns can take.

Part Two will show you how to use these pronouns in sentences. Pronouns can do the same jobs that nouns do, but their forms are different. Since pronouns are substitutes for nouns, many concepts already covered in Chapter 1 are repeated here. This review will enable you to strengthen your comprehension of some of the fundamental concepts of the English language.

Here is a summary of the material about the forms and uses of pronouns covered in this chapter.

Part One
What Information Do Pronouns Give?

Uses of Pronouns
Personal Pronouns
Grammar Person of Pronouns
Number of Pronouns
Gender of Pronouns

Part Two
What Jobs Can Pronouns Do?

Pronouns as Subjects
Pronouns as Direct Objects
Pronouns as Objects of Prepositions
Possessive Pronouns
Pronouns as Question Words

PART ONE
What Information Do Pronouns Give?

3.2 Pronoun Chart

The following chart gives an overview of the most common uses of pronouns.

Common Uses of Pronouns

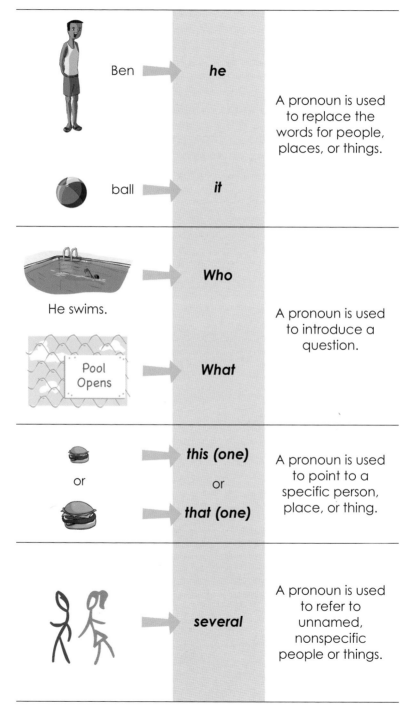

Ben →	*he*	A pronoun is used to replace the words for people, places, or things.
ball →	*it*	
He swims. →	*Who*	A pronoun is used to introduce a question.
Pool Opens →	*What*	
or →	*this (one)* or *that (one)*	A pronoun is used to point to a specific person, place, or thing.
→	*several*	A pronoun is used to refer to unnamed, nonspecific people or things.

3.3 Pronouns Avoid Repetition

**Pronouns can be used in place of
nouns to avoid monotonous repetition.**

You will often want to refer to the same noun a number of times
within connected sentences. The following example illustrates
how the noun **Susan** is used several times.

Nouns — **Susan** goes to the pool.

Susan works at Lakewood Pool.

Ben asks **Susan** if **Susan** wants a party.

Nouns

The use of another part of speech—pronouns—can avoid
repetition:

Noun — **Susan** goes to the pool.

Pronoun — **She** works at Lakewood Pool.

Ben asks **her** if **she** wants a party.

Pronouns

The most common task for pronouns is replacing nouns. Like the
nouns they replace, pronouns refer to people, places, or things.

3.4 Personal Pronouns

Of the various types of pronouns, the most common are the
personal pronouns: **I, you, he, she, it, we, they**. These pronouns
are called *personal* because they refer most often to people,
although they can also refer to things.

**A *personal pronoun* is a pronoun used to replace
words for people, places, or things.**

The characteristics found in most personal pronouns refer to
number, gender, and grammar person. A pronoun's form provides
information about these characteristics.

You are familiar with the concepts of number and gender of
English nouns (see Chapter 1). Now you will learn to apply the

concepts of number and gender to pronouns, as well as to learn a new concept—*grammar person.*

> **Form refers to the qualities and characteristics that pronouns have in common.**

3.5 Grammar Person

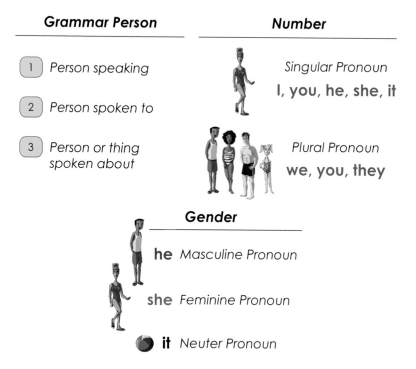

Grammar Person	**Number**

1. Person speaking

2. Person spoken to

3. Person or thing spoken about

Singular Pronoun
I, you, he, she, it

Plural Pronoun
we, you, they

Gender

he Masculine Pronoun

she Feminine Pronoun

it Neuter Pronoun

The concept of *grammar person* is one of the most important concepts of this chapter. In Chapter 4, Verbs, you will also see how this concept is used when conjugating verbs.

A personal pronoun shows by its form whether it refers to the person speaking, the person spoken to, or the person or thing spoken about.

> **Every personal pronoun is classified by whether it is first, second, or third person.**

Grammar Person	Singular	Plural

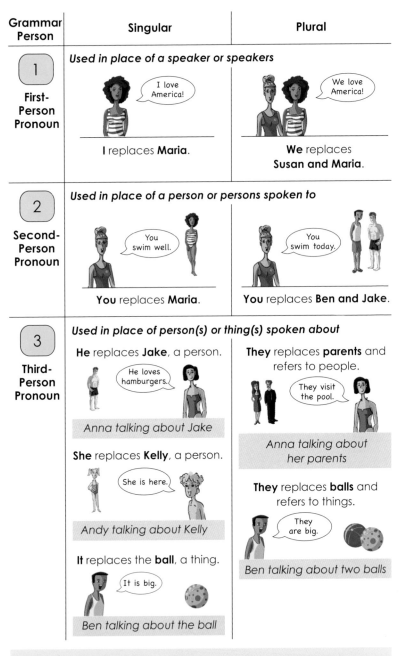

1 First-Person Pronoun	*Used in place of a speaker or speakers* I love America! **I** replaces **Maria**.	We love America! **We** replaces **Susan and Maria**.
2 Second-Person Pronoun	*Used in place of a person or persons spoken to* You swim well. **You** replaces **Maria**.	You swim today. **You** replaces **Ben and Jake**.
3 Third-Person Pronoun	*Used in place of person(s) or thing(s) spoken about* **He** replaces **Jake**, a person. He loves hamburgers. *Anna talking about Jake* **She** replaces **Kelly**, a person. She is here. *Andy talking about Kelly* **It** replaces the **ball**, a thing. It is big. *Ben talking about the ball*	**They** replaces **parents** and refers to people. They visit the pool. *Anna talking about her parents* **They** replaces **balls** and refers to things. They are big. *Ben talking about two balls*

Personal pronouns refer to persons. The exceptions are the pronoun "it," which refers to inanimate things, and the pronoun "they," which sometimes refers to inanimate things.

3.6 Number of Pronouns

**Personal pronouns show
either singular or plural number.**

When you look at the chart on the opposite page, you see
that the pronouns listed on the left refer to one person or thing,
whereas those on the right indicate more than one person
or thing.

If you classify pronouns based on number, you can divide them
as illustrated below:

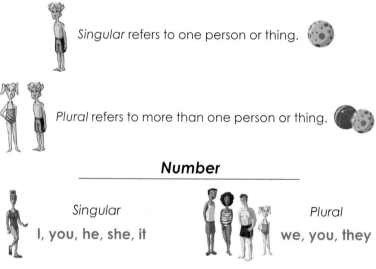

Singular refers to one person or thing.

Plural refers to more than one person or thing.

Number

Singular	*Plural*
I, you, he, she, it	we, you, they

Each pronoun in the singular group stands for only one person
or one thing. In Chapter 4, Verbs, these details about pronouns
become important when you have to decide whether to use a
singular verb form or a plural verb form.

The pronoun **you** has a double role. The context in the sentence
will indicate whether **you** is used as a singular or as a plural
pronoun. The pronoun **they** also has a double role. It can refer
to people or to things, provided there is more than one.

The third-person singular includes three pronouns. Remember
the shortcut "three in three": *3* pronouns (*he, she, it*) in *3rd*
person. In Chapter 4, you will connect pronouns to verb forms,
so it is important that you understand pronouns well before
you move on.

*Now that we've covered **person** and **number**, let's take a closer look at the **gender** of pronouns. Remember masculine, feminine, and neuter nouns from Chapter 1? Since pronouns take the place of nouns, you will also find masculine, feminine, and neuter pronouns, but you need to learn how to identify them.*

3.7 Gender of Pronouns

Three genders differentiate the third-person singular pronouns "he," "she," and "it."

Gender

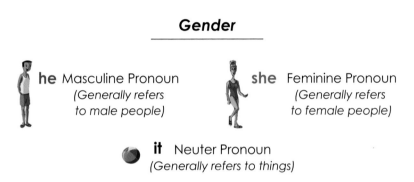

he Masculine Pronoun
(Generally refers to male people)

she Feminine Pronoun
(Generally refers to female people)

it Neuter Pronoun
(Generally refers to things)

We say "generally" here because pronouns do not always follow these simple rules: Animals are classified as male or female, and sometimes inanimate objects (such as ships and boats) are referred to as *she*. Here are examples for each of the three genders:

Masculine Nouns
Mr. Miller
man
father
actor
bull

Replace each noun with pronoun
he

Feminine Nouns
Mrs. Miller
woman
mother
actress
cow

Replace each noun with pronoun
she

Neuter Nouns
locker
ball
towel
lotion

Replace each noun with pronoun
it

Note: Because most nouns can be replaced by third-person pronouns, we sometimes speak of nouns as being in the third person also.

> ## Gender does not differentiate
> ## the pronouns "I," "you," "we," and "they."

The pronouns **I**, **you**, **he**, **she**, and **it** replace singular nouns, but only the third-person forms differentiate gender. The pronouns **we**, **you**, and **they** replace plural nouns, and none of the plural pronouns differentiate gender.

The chart below shows singular and plural personal pronouns for all three persons, and highlights the double role that the pronoun **they** can have, replacing nouns for both people and things. Even when **they** refers to people, it does not differentiate gender. **They** can refer to both males and females.

Personal Pronouns

| Person | Number | |
	Singular	Plural
First Person	① I	① we
Second Person	② you	② you
Third Person	③ he, she, **it**	③ **they**

Replace Singular Nouns   *Replace Plural Nouns*

they

they
People   or   Things
the boys the girls the flippers

3.8 Another Personal Pronoun: Possessive Pronouns

> ## A pronoun used to show possession
> ## is called a *possessive pronoun.*

You have learned that a possessive noun establishes a relationship between the owner and what is being owned. The form of the pronouns **mine**, **yours**, **his**, **hers**, **its**, **ours**, **yours**, and **theirs** also indicates a relationship to a person or thing.

45

As the following examples indicate, these possessive pronouns show that same relationship in only one word.

Possessive Pronouns

		Possessive Pronouns
It is mine.	The speaker, Anna, talking about her hula hoop	First-person pronoun **mine** referring to the speaker (**I**)
Yes, it is yours.	Jake speaking to Anna, talking about her hula hoop	Second-person pronoun **yours** referring to the person spoken to (**you**)
Yes, it is hers.	Ben talking about Anna's hula hoop	Third-person pronoun **hers** referring to the person spoken about (**she**, or Anna)

Part Two of this chapter will offer more details about the use of pronouns. As we conclude this section about personal pronouns, look at the noun-pronoun examples given with each image.

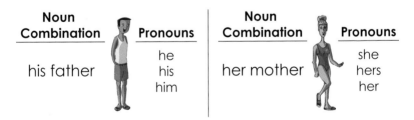

Noun Combination		Pronouns	Noun Combination		Pronouns
his father		he his him	her mother		she hers her

Many possessive forms can play a double role: They can be used as adjectives in combination with nouns, but as pronouns, they stand alone. Possessive adjectives, including **his** and **her**, are explained in detail in Chapter 2, Adjectives.

3.9 Pronouns Used to Form Questions

A pronoun is often used to introduce a question.

Susan swims. **Who** swims?
/   \
Noun   *Pronoun*

The pool opens. **What** opens?
/   \
Noun   *Pronoun*

Pool Opens Today!

Who *and* **What** *are question words. You will learn more about the jobs they have to do in Part Two.*

3.10 Pronouns Pointing Out People or Things

A pronoun can be used to point to specific persons, places, or things.

This, **that**, **these**, and **those** are pronouns commonly used to point out people, places, or things without naming them. As pronouns, they stand alone. However, in context, they must refer to someone or something that has already been mentioned. They often indicate the location of people or things as being near or far from the speaker. In form, they can show number, as illustrated in the next example.

*Singular Pronouns refer to **one** person or thing*

this (one) or **that (one)**

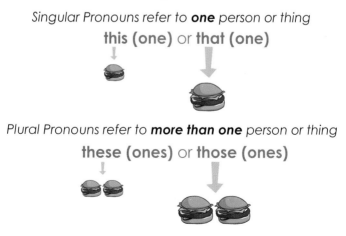

*Plural Pronouns refer to **more than one** person or thing*

these (ones) or **those (ones)**

3.11 Pronouns Naming Nonspecific People or Things

> **A pronoun is often used to refer to unnamed, nonspecific persons or things.**

These pronouns refer to people, places, or things in general. By looking at their form, you can see whether these pronouns refer to one or many.

Singular pronouns refer to a person or thing: **each, somebody, something**, or **anything**.

Plural pronouns refer to more than one person or thing: **both, several, few**, or **many**.

Somebody always takes the flippers.

*The pronoun **somebody** refers to an unnamed person. We don't know if it is a boy or a girl.*

Something happened at the pool.

*The pronoun **something** can refer to an accident or a celebration. We don't know which.*

Several came to the swim meet.

*The pronoun **several** indicates unspecified people attending the swim meet.*

There are many different pronouns in this category. Only a few are listed here. Look at the examples to understand what they all have in common: They refer to people or things without naming them.

PART TWO
What Jobs Can Pronouns Do?

3.12 Overview: Subject Pronouns, Object Pronouns, and Possessive Pronouns

The roles pronouns can play divide them into three distinct groups: subject pronouns, object pronouns, and possessive pronouns.

Subject Pronoun		Object Pronoun		Possessive Pronoun	
Replaces noun— person(s) or thing(s)		*Replaces noun— person(s) or thing(s)*		*Replaces noun— person(s) or thing(s)*	
Subject Noun	*Subject Pronoun*	*Object Noun*	*Object Pronoun*	*Possessive Noun*	*Possessive Pronoun*
Ben	he	**Ben**	him	**Ben's**	his
Maria	she	**Maria**	her	**Maria's**	hers

You have already learned in Part One that the form of a pronoun gives information about grammar person, number, and gender:

Person: First person (speaking), second person (spoken to), or third person (spoken about)

Number: singular (one in number) or plural (more than one)

Gender: masculine, feminine, or neuter

The role played by a pronoun in the sentence determines whether a subject pronoun, an object pronoun, or a possessive pronoun is used.

The following charts show person, number, and gender for the three groups of pronouns.

						Masculine	Feminine	Neuter
Subject Pronouns	*Singular*	①	I	②	you	③ he	she	it
	Plural	①	we	②	you	③ they		
	A subject pronoun performs the action of the verb.							

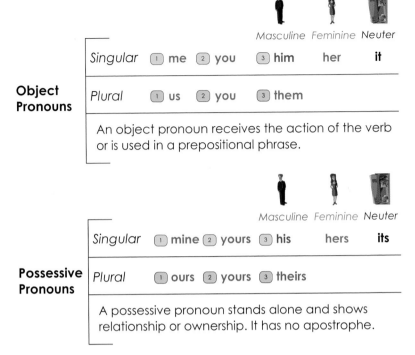

Object Pronouns

				Masculine	Feminine	Neuter
Singular	① me	② you	③ him		her	**it**
Plural	① us	② you	③ them			

An object pronoun receives the action of the verb or is used in a prepositional phrase.

Possessive Pronouns

				Masculine	Feminine	Neuter
Singular	① mine	② yours	③ his		hers	**its**
Plural	① ours	② yours	③ theirs			

A possessive pronoun stands alone and shows relationship or ownership. It has no apostrophe.

The next section will illustrate subject and object pronouns.
Charts show you where to find the matching pronouns.

3.13 A Great Start: Subject Pronouns

A *subject pronoun* identifies what the sentence is all about.

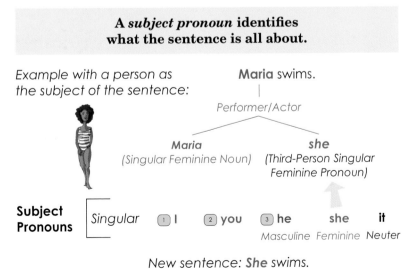

Example with a person as the subject of the sentence:

Maria swims.

Performer/Actor

Maria
(Singular Feminine Noun)

she
(Third-Person Singular Feminine Pronoun)

Subject Pronouns

Singular	① I	② you	③ he	she	**it**
			Masculine	Feminine	Neuter

New sentence: **She** swims.

50

In the sentence **Maria swims**, the subject **Maria** is replaced with the pronoun **she**. The new sentence is **She swims**. This example illustrates how the selection of an appropriate pronoun to replace a noun depends on knowing the noun's person (third person, because Maria is being spoken about), number (singular, because there is only one Maria), and gender (feminine, because Maria is a girl). **She** is the feminine third-person singular pronoun that stands for **Maria**.

Apply the same analysis in the next example, where the subject is a thing.

Example with a thing as the subject of the sentence:

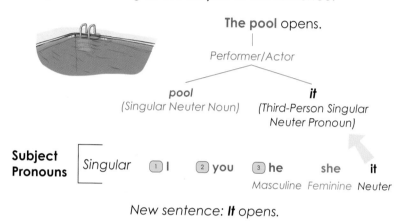

*New sentence: **It** opens.*

In the next section, the sentences become longer and include an object.

3.14 Subject and Object Pronouns Together

Verbs play a central role in a sentence. The subject connects to the verb. When extending the sentence to include an object, it is the verb that makes it possible. The following section, therefore, discusses subject pronouns and object pronouns together.

> **A *direct object pronoun* receives the action of the verb. The verb in this type of sentence is called an *action verb*.**

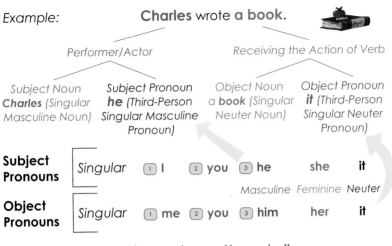

Example: **Charles wrote a book.**

New sentence: **He** wrote **it.**

Charles is the subject in this sentence. The subject pronoun **he** refers to **Charles**. The action verb **wrote** takes **book** as an object, because the noun **book** receives the action of the verb **wrote**. The object pronoun refers to **book**.

It can have a double role. In the earlier example **The pool opens**, the pronoun **it** replaces the subject (**The pool**). In the example above, **He wrote it**, the pronoun **it** refers to the direct object (**a book**). Because pronouns can have the same form whether used as subjects or objects, it is important to identify the subject first and then determine the object of the sentence.

The next example shows a plural subject.

Example:

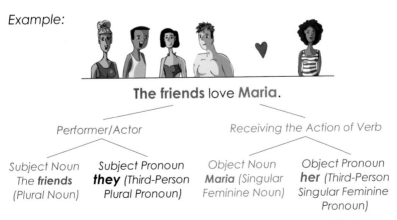

The friends love Maria.

The following chart of subject and object pronouns highlights the pronouns used as replacements for nouns in this example.

Subject Pronouns			Object Pronouns		

Singular	Plural	Singular	Plural
① I	① we	① me	① us
② you	② you	② you	② you
③ he, she, it	③ **they**	③ him, **her**, it	③ them

*New sentence: **They** love **her**.*

The replacement for this plural subject noun, **the friends**, is the plural pronoun **they**.

In this example, the noun **Maria** is the object of the verb **love**. **Maria**, as a singular noun, must be replaced with a third-person singular pronoun. Here, the feminine form of the third-person object pronoun (**her**) replaces the feminine noun **Maria**.

Example:

Maria loves **them**.

Maria is the subject of the sentence. The pronoun **them** receives the action of the verb **love**. **Them** is a third-person plural object pronoun that replaces the noun **friends**.

Remember: Direct objects need action verbs. More details about action verbs are given in Chapter 4.

3.15 A Different Job: Object Pronouns with Prepositions

Object pronouns are also used with prepositions.

You have learned that action verbs and direct object pronouns go together. The direct object receives the action of the verb. The object pronouns **me, you, him, her, it, us, you,** and **them** are also used with prepositions. Each one of them can be used to complete a prepositional phrase.

Example: Ben stands **under the lifeguard chair.**

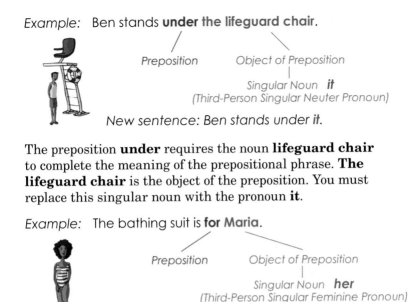

Preposition   Object of Preposition
                            |
                   Singular Noun   **it**
           (Third-Person Singular Neuter Pronoun)

New sentence: Ben stands under it.

The preposition **under** requires the noun **lifeguard chair** to complete the meaning of the prepositional phrase. **The lifeguard chair** is the object of the preposition. You must replace this singular noun with the pronoun **it.**

Example: The bathing suit is **for Maria.**

Preposition   Object of Preposition
                            |
                   Singular Noun   **her**
         (Third-Person Singular Feminine Pronoun)

*New sentence: The bathing suit is for **her.***

3.16 Possessive Pronouns

A *possessive pronoun* shows relationship or ownership.

Look again at the example that appeared on page 46 in Part One.

Possessive Pronoun

Yes, it is hers. Ben talking about Anna's hula hoop	Third-person pronoun **hers** referring to the person spoken about (**she,** or Anna)

Let's take another look at subject pronouns, and then we'll move on to possessive pronouns.

		Masculine	Feminine	Neuter
Subject Pronouns	*Singular* ① I ② you ③ he	she	it
	Plural ① we ② you ③ they		

54

		Masculine	Feminine	Neuter
Possessive Pronouns	*Singular*	① mine ② yours ③ his	hers	**its**
	Plural	① ours ② yours ③ theirs		

Possessive pronouns are based on the subject pronouns and indicate the person or persons to whom they refer. Possessive pronouns stand alone, like all the other pronouns covered so far. In the example **it is hers**, **hers** refers to Anna's hula hoop. An apostrophe is used with a possessive noun, but never with a possessive pronoun.

3.17 Question Words Revisited

The question words **Who** and **What** were introduced in Part One. Pronouns used as question words have several jobs to do. They are used to identify both subjects and objects. Let's take a closer look at question words asking about subjects.

Question Words Asking About the Subject

The question word "Who" is used to identify a person acting as a subject. The question word "What" is used to identify an inanimate object (thing) or animal acting as a subject.

You can use the question word **Who** to identify a person referred to by a subject noun or pronoun. **What** takes the place of a subject noun or pronoun when it refers to an inanimate thing.

Examples:

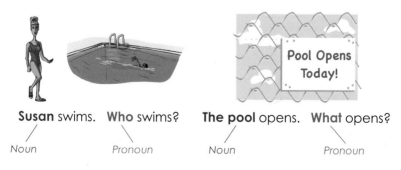

Susan swims. **Who** swims?
/ \
Noun   Pronoun

The pool opens. **What** opens?
/ \
Noun   Pronoun

55

Question Words Asking About the Object

The question word "Who" changes to "Whom" when asking about an object.

Examples:

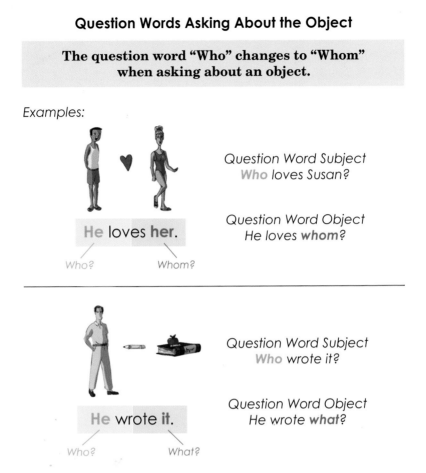

Question Word Subject
Who loves Susan?

Question Word Object
*He loves **whom**?*

Question Word Subject
Who wrote it?

Question Word Object
*He wrote **what**?*

What plays a double role. Use **What** to identify either an inanimate subject or an inanimate object.

Question Word Asking About a Possessive Noun

The question word "Whose" is used to identify possession or ownership.

Example:

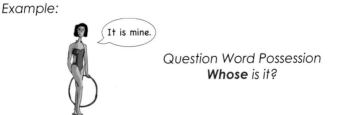

It is mine.

Question Word Possession
***Whose** is it?*

3.18 Overview of Pronouns

Congratulations! You have now learned how to replace nouns with pronouns to make more interesting sentences. At the conclusion of Chapter 1, Nouns, we introduced the Venn diagram with the noun **trophy**. This overview uses the same sentences, but replaces the noun **trophy** with the appropriate pronoun.

Venn Diagram

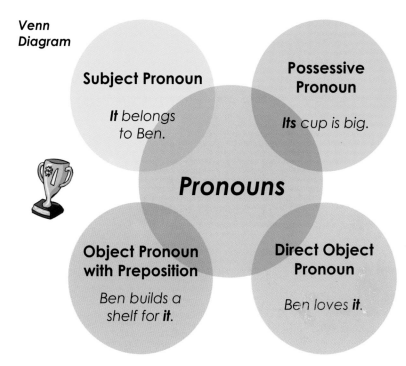

Remember, the noun chapter concluded with the following review phrases and sentences: **Maria swims**, **Maria's bathing suit**, **Anna loves Maria**, and **The gift is for Maria**. We'll now conclude the pronoun chapter using the same examples except with pronouns replacing the nouns. Keep in mind that pronouns are always substitutes for nouns!

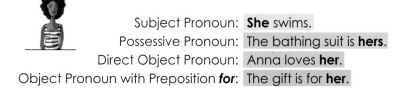

Subject Pronoun: **She** swims.
Possessive Pronoun: The bathing suit is **hers**.
Direct Object Pronoun: Anna loves **her**.
Object Pronoun with Preposition *for*: The gift is for **her**.

3.19 Review Exercises

A Determine whether the pronoun in red type is in first, second, or third person. Write **1st** if it is a first-person pronoun, **2nd** if it is a second-person pronoun, or **3rd** if it is a third-person pronoun.

1. They watch television. _____
2. We want ice cream. _____
3. You sing well. _____
4. I am tired. _____
5. She is my friend. _____

B Determine whether the pronoun in red type is singular or plural. Write **S** for singular or **P** for plural.

1. Somebody lives there. _____
2. These are good! _____
3. Do they like the movie? _____
4. He is in college. _____
5. I have a pet dog. _____
6. We like the teacher. _____
7. Both are at the pool. _____

C Determine whether or not the pronoun in red type is possessive. Write **P** if it is possessive or **X** if it is not possessive.

1. The cat is not hers. _____
2. She does not play soccer. _____
3. Who wrote the letter? _____
4. The book is mine. _____
5. His bathing suit is blue. _____
6. Nobody is at the pool. _____

D Determine whether the pronoun in red type is a subject pronoun or an object pronoun. Write **SP** if it is a subject pronoun or **OP** if it is an object pronoun.

1. He throws the ball. _____
2. To whom is he speaking? _____
3. They talk to me. _____
4. You are pretty. _____
5. He gives candy to us. _____
6. She sends postcards to them. _____
7. We do not want to run. _____

E Complete each sentence with the appropriate pronoun from the choices given.

1. _____ is yellow. (What | Her | It)
2. To _____ does he talk? (yours | whom | these)
3. The cookies are _____. (ours | she | them)
4. _____ am tall. (What | Its | I)
5. _____ belong to me. (Those | He | It)
6. Give the money to _____. (yours | her | we)

CHAPTER 4

VERBS

4.1 Part One and Part Two Overview

The *verb* is the most fundamental part of speech. Only verbs can make a statement about the subject.

Every sentence must have a verb.

This chapter takes a close look at all the jobs verbs can perform. You will also learn the names given to each type of verb. This will help you to identify and use each verb correctly and effectively. Here is a summary of the material about the forms and uses of verbs covered in this chapter.

Part One: Form of English Verbs
Verb Basics

Verb Families
Types of Verbs
Regular and Irregular Verbs
The Four Principal Parts

Part Two: Uses of English Verbs
The Four Principal Parts and Verb Tenses

Modals: Special Helping Verbs
Linking and Non-Action Verbs as Main Verbs
Verbs in Questions and Statements
Verbs Taking Objects
Verbs Expressing Commands

4.2 Verb Families

The Miller Family

A family's name is important to any family. It includes all the members of that family. Verbs also have families. Each verb family has many different parts that belong within the family. In grammar, we call the family name of a verb its *infinitive form*.

> The *infinitive form* consists of the word "to" plus the base form of a verb.

Here are three examples of the infinitive form:

to eat   to swim   to write

Because verbs can take many different forms, knowing the verb's family name makes it much easier to use verbs correctly. As a next step, we will cover the different types of verbs you need to be able to recognize.

4.3 Types of Verbs

> A verb is a word showing or expressing *action, being,* or *state of being.*

What kind of action does a verb show? Some verbs show physical action.

Action Verbs

Examples: to eat   to swim   to write

> *Action verbs* express the action, often physical action,
> that the subject does.

Non-Action Verbs

Here are three examples of non-action verbs: **to think, to look,**
and **to understand.**

> *Non-action verbs* tell about states of mind or senses.
> They do not express physical action.

Linking Verbs

You learned about *linking verbs* in Chapter 1, Nouns.

> *Linking verbs* convey a state of being.
> They link the subject of a sentence with a word
> that renames or describes the subject.

A State of Being

| Susan is the winner. | The pool is warm. | Mr. Smith is the manager of the pool. |

While the most common linking verb is **to be**, there are other
linking verbs you will need to know, such as **to appear, to
become, to feel, to grow, to look,** and **to taste.**

To be is the most important linking verb. In this chapter, the
following forms of the verb **to be** appear in examples: **am, are,
is, was,** and **were.**

Helping Verbs

Verbs often use other verbs in sentences. Although a main verb represents the important idea of the sentence, it may need a helper to express its full meaning. Here are the forms of three helping verbs that appear in this chapter:

to be	***am, are, is, was, were***
to do	***do, does, did***
to have	***have, has, had***

Could, **would**, and **must** are examples of a special kind of helping verb that will be explained later in this chapter.

The following explanation of these helping verbs will make it easier to sort out how they do their jobs.

> ***Helping verbs*** **help the main verb to make a statement, ask a question, or give a command.**

Verbs are complex; we include here the essential information for understanding verbs and how to use them. You will find the following short definition of verbs helpful.

> **A *verb* is a word that tells what the subject of a sentence does, experiences, or owns.**

The next section will cover the two main verb groups that you need to understand before we explain the principal parts of verbs.

4.4 Regular and Irregular Verbs

Verbs change in form. Based on how they change, verbs are divided into two groups.

One group of verbs uses a predictable pattern in changing form.

You will see this pattern in the four examples of the verb **watch**:

Regular Verb Examples:

Today I **watch** the race.
I **am watching** the race.
Yesterday I **watched** the race.
I **have watched** the race every day.

This first group of verbs is called *regular verbs*. All regular verbs display the same pattern of predictable changes.

The second group does not follow a regular pattern. Verb forms in this group change for no apparent reason. There is no obvious pattern you can apply when learning them.

Irregular Verb Examples:

We **eat** hamburgers.
We **are eating** hamburgers.
Yesterday we **ate** hamburgers.
We **have eaten** hamburgers every day.

This second group includes verbs that are not regular. They are called *irregular verbs*.

> **All verbs in the English language**
> **can be divided into two groups:**
> *regular verbs* **and** *irregular* **verbs.**

Most English verbs are regular. Irregular verbs have verb forms that require memorization before you can use them correctly. There is no easy way to explain their changes and no way to avoid memorizing their verb forms.

Let's use what we have learned so far to build sentences.

4.5 The Four Principal Parts of a Verb

When you want to express an idea, you usually start with a noun or pronoun that will become the subject of your sentence. Once you know your subject, you need to state what the subject does.

Every sentence must have a subject and a verb.

Verbs can take many different forms. In English grammar, there is a system for all the different verb forms you might want to use when building sentences: *The Four Principal Parts of a Verb*. It is a framework that will help you to correctly make or identify the different forms of verbs you might need to express your ideas.

All English verbs have four principal parts.

The following example shows the four principal parts of the verb **to go**.

Examples:

Maria goes to the pool.
Maria **went** to the pool.
Maria **is going** to the pool.
Maria has gone to the pool.

The word *principal* in the term *principal parts* tells you that these verb forms represent main forms common to all verbs.

We will first explain the form of each principal part. Once you know their names and understand the form of each of the principal parts here, it will be much easier to understand how to use them with verb tenses in Part Two.

4.6 The First Principal Part: Base Form

Before we start, keep in mind what verbs can do. How do you identify a verb? The following will help you remember the job verbs perform in a sentence.

A verb is one or more words answering the question "What is happening?" or "What did happen?"

Now, these are base forms of the verbs **to write, to eat, to swim,** and **to love**.

write   eat   swim   love

**The *base form* of a verb is a verb without
any endings added.**

The *base form* of a verb allows the beginning language learner
to form basic sentences with a subject and a verb. As Part Two
will explain in detail, it is used to express an action that
happens in the *present* moment.

Principal Part ⟨1⟩ , the base form of a verb, connects to a subject.
The following chart illustrates how verb forms change when
they are combined with matching subject pronouns.

Subject as Pronoun		Connecting Verb	Sentence
 ⟨1⟩	I	swim	I swim.
 ⟨2⟩	you	swim	You swim.
 ⟨3⟩	he she it	swims	He swims. She swims. It swims.
 ⟨1⟩	we	swim	We swim.
 ⟨2⟩	you	swim	You swim.
 ⟨3⟩	they	swim	They swim.

As was explained in Chapter 3, pronouns are grouped into first, second, and third persons. Let's take a closer look at singular pronouns.

The singular pronouns are **I, you, he, she,** and **it.** These pronouns stand for one person only. As the chart indicates, no changes occur in the first person (**I**), nor in the second person (**you**). However, the third person of singular pronouns is divided into the pronouns **he, she,** and **it.**

The connecting verb differs from the base form of the verb in the third-person singular only.

Third-Person Singular Subject Pronoun	Third-Person Singular Verb Form	Base Form of Verb	Infinitive Form of Verb
He	**writes** a book.	write	to write
She	**sits** in the lifeguard chair.	sit	to sit
He	**fixes** the locker.	fix	to fix
It	**opens** at 9:00.	open	to open
She	**studies** English.	study	to study

The majority of verbs follow the regular pattern of using the base form of a verb to connect to a subject. The third-person singular is an exception to this rule.

In the chart above, the verb forms change when they are connected to the singular subject pronouns **he, she,** and **it.** Recognizing and using these verb changes are important for learning the basics of the English language.

Learn to look at the final letters of the base form of the verb to identify what changes are necessary for the third-person singular. Here is a basic guide:

Most verbs	Base form + **-s**	*He eats.*
Verbs ending in **-ch, -s, -x,** or **-z**	Base form + **-es**	*He fixes.*
Verbs ending in **-y**	Base form – **-y** + **-ies**	*Maria studies.*

Subjects: Pronouns and Nouns

Remember: When forming a sentence, you always have the choice of connecting the verb to either a pronoun or a noun.

> **If the subject noun or pronoun is singular, use a singular verb. If the subject noun or pronoun is plural, use a plural verb.**

He, **she**, or **it** can be replaced by a singular noun, and **they** by a plural noun. Likewise, a singular noun can be replaced by **he**, **she**, or **it**, and a plural noun by **they**.

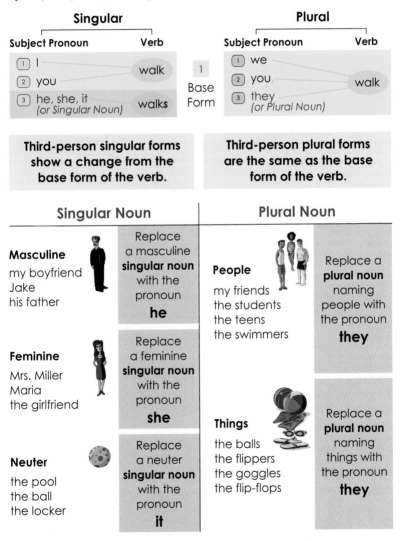

Singular

Subject Pronoun	Verb
① I	walk
② you	
③ he, she, it (or Singular Noun)	walks

1 Base Form

Third-person singular forms show a change from the base form of the verb.

Plural

Subject Pronoun	Verb
① we	
② you	walk
③ they (or Plural Noun)	

Third-person plural forms are the same as the base form of the verb.

Singular Noun		Plural Noun	
Masculine my boyfriend Jake his father	Replace a masculine **singular noun** with the pronoun **he**	**People** my friends the students the teens the swimmers	Replace a **plural noun** naming people with the pronoun **they**
Feminine Mrs. Miller Maria the girlfriend	Replace a feminine **singular noun** with the pronoun **she**	**Things** the balls the flippers the goggles the flip-flops	Replace a **plural noun** naming things with the pronoun **they**
Neuter the pool the ball the locker	Replace a neuter **singular noun** with the pronoun **it**		

The vast number of nouns you could choose as subjects is too big for this book. However, verbs can also connect to pronouns. Since you know how to replace nouns with pronouns, we will simplify the presentation of the principal parts of verbs by using pronouns for most of the examples.

In Part Two you will learn that verbs show time. We have covered the verb form used to make general statements. It is identical to the base form of the verb except that we had to make a small change for the third-person singular. The principal part that we will look at next is a verb form that expresses action that took place in the past.

4.7 The Second Principal Part: Past Form 2

It is a good practice to always start with the base form of a verb. Both regular and irregular verbs can show changes in their forms. The changes for regular verbs build on the base form, and these changes are easily recognized. When irregular verbs change their form, however, the base form can be very hard to detect. Therefore, it is essential for beginners to learn the base form of verbs.

Principal Part 2 is the past form of verbs. The following examples illustrate changing from the base form to the past form of both regular and irregular verbs.

I walked to the school.

Base form: walk

The past form of a regular verb follows a pattern: Add **-ed** to the base form of the verb.

I wrote a book.

Base form: write

The past form of an irregular verb follows no apparent pattern: The past form must be memorized.

Regular verbs follow a set pattern of adding "-ed" to the base form when forming the past form of a verb.

Here are examples of the base form and past form of three regular verbs: fix ~ fix**ed**, match ~ match**ed**, learn ~ learn**ed**.

Note these spelling changes when adding the suffix **-ed**: study ~ stud**ied**, trim ~ trim**med**.

71

Past forms of irregular verbs change their forms without following a pattern.

Irregular verbs in the past form can be tricky. Memorizing all the forms of irregular verbs is essential.

Here are examples of the base form and past form of three irregular verbs: go ~ **went**, say ~ **said**, win ~ **won**.

I won!

The past form of a verb does not change according to the subject it is connected to.

The chart for Past Form on the next page shows that one past form connects to all subject pronouns. The examples **walked**, **wrote**, **went**, and **said** include both regular and irregular verbs. Each of these verbs is a main verb.

*For the next two principal parts, the same main verbs are used again, but they need the company of **helping verbs**.*

4.8 The Third Principal Part: Present Participle `3`

Look at the flippers. They are a swimming device. Are they doing the swimming for you? No, they are just helpers when swimming. Helping verbs work the same way. The helping verb is there to help the main verb. It is the main verb that tells you what the important message is.

***Helping verbs* help the main verb tell about an action or make a statement.**

Principal Part `3` is called the *present participle*. The present participle of the main verb is used with a form of the helping verb **to be**.

The following examples illustrate how **am, are,** and **is**—all forms of the helping verb **to be**—combine with the present participle in a sentence.

Susan **is walking** around the pool.

Helping Verb   *Present Participle*
                              (Main Verb)

72

I **am** swimming.

Helping Verb   Present Participle
              (Main Verb)

We **are** celebrating.

Helping Verb   Present Participle
              (Main Verb)

To form the present participle, you start with the base form of a regular or irregular verb. However, there are several spelling changes to keep in mind:

Add **-ing** to the base form of the verb: walk ~ walk**ing**.
If a verb ends in a silent **-e**, drop the final **-e** and add **-ing**: write ~ writ**ing**.
In one-syllable verbs, the final consonant is often doubled: swim ~ swim**ming**.
Do not double the consonants **w**, **x**, or **y**: play ~ play**ing**.

Swimming and **celebrating** are examples of present participles. Present participles don't change when they connect to **am**, **are**, and **is**. They are not able to stand alone, but they are connected to a form of the helping verb **to be**.

A verb may consist of more than one word. A main verb and a helping verb together form a _verb phrase_.

The following two charts contrast past forms (Principal Part **2**) with present participles (Principal Part **3**). Past forms of verbs stand alone as one word, while present participles (the **-ing** form) need a helping verb. It is the helping verb that connects to the subject and changes according to the subject. The present participle is the main verb, and it doesn't change.

2   Past Form

Subject Pronoun	Past Form
① I	
② you	
③ he, she, it (or Singular Noun)	walked
① we	
② you	
③ they (or Plural Noun)	

3   Present Participle

Subject Pronoun	Helping Verb	Present Participle
① I	am	
② you	are	
③ he, she, it (or Singular Noun)	is	walking
① we	are	
② you	are	
③ they (or Plural Noun)	are	

The term *present participle* refers to an action in the present. As we move to the next principal part, you will find that the word *past* in the term *past participle* indicates an action that already took place. Keep this distinction in mind when we cover *verb tenses*.

4.9 The Fourth Principal Part: Past Participle 4

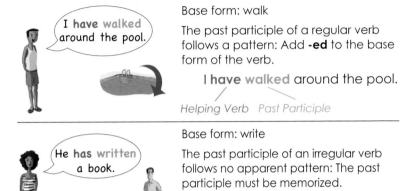

Base form: walk

The past participle of a regular verb follows a pattern: Add **-ed** to the base form of the verb.

I **have** walked around the pool.

／　＼

Helping Verb　Past Participle

Base form: write

The past participle of an irregular verb follows no apparent pattern: The past participle must be memorized.

He **has** written a book.

／　＼

Helping Verb　Past Participle

Walked and **written** are two examples of past participles. As past participles, they need a helping verb to be complete. For past participles, the helping verb is **to have**. The forms used with the examples above are **have** and **has**. As the second example shows, the third-person singular verb form changes from **have** to **has** when it connects to **he, she,** or **it**.

Have walked and **have written** are two examples of *verb phrases*. They each have a helping verb and a main verb.

Here is a short overview of the four principal parts based on the two verbs used throughout Part One.

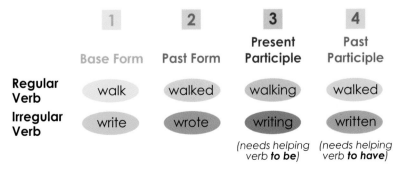

	1 Base Form	2 Past Form	3 Present Participle	4 Past Participle
Regular Verb	walk	walked	walking	walked
Irregular Verb	write	wrote	writing	written
			*(needs helping verb **to be**)*	*(needs helping verb **to have**)*

At the end of this chapter, you will find a complete overview of
the four principal parts of a verb.

PART TWO: USES OF ENGLISH VERBS
4.10 The Four Principal Parts and Verb Tenses

**Verbs express time. Tenses reflect the time
expressed by a verb.**

The four principal parts are all about tenses, that is, the time
when the action takes place. In Part One, you learned about
the form of these four principal parts. Now, in Part Two, you
will learn how the four principal parts are used to express time.
The four principal parts correspond to the following five tenses.

1	2	3	4
Present Tense	Past	Present	Present
Future Tense	Tense	Continuous	Perfect

**There are three periods in time:
present (*now*), past (*yesterday*), and future (*tomorrow*).**

Now is used with the present tense, **yesterday** with the past
tense (the simple past), and **tomorrow** with the future tense
(the simple future). These are basic tenses for any beginning
language learner.

These tenses build on what you have learned about the four
principal parts of a verb. Like the present tense, the future
tense uses Principal Part 1 , the base form of a verb. You might
be surprised to find two present tenses and two past tenses.
We will contrast each pair with examples that illustrate how
verbs express time in many different ways.

The chart on the following page shows three people.
Each one expresses different ideas. As you read
them, try to find out how the verb forms indicate
when or *at what time* these actions take place.
Ask the following questions: Is it happening now,
did it happen yesterday, or has it yet to take place?

Verbs Express Time

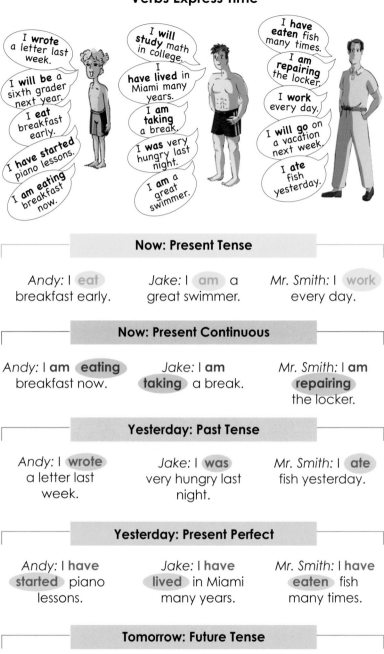

Now: Present Tense

Andy: I eat breakfast early.

Jake: I am a great swimmer.

Mr. Smith: I work every day.

Now: Present Continuous

Andy: I **am eating** breakfast now.

Jake: I **am taking** a break.

Mr. Smith: I **am repairing** the locker.

Yesterday: Past Tense

Andy: I wrote a letter last week.

Jake: I was very hungry last night.

Mr. Smith: I ate fish yesterday.

Yesterday: Present Perfect

Andy: I **have started** piano lessons.

Jake: I **have lived** in Miami many years.

Mr. Smith: I **have eaten** fish many times.

Tomorrow: Future Tense

Andy: I **will be** a sixth grader next year.

Jake: I **will study** math in college.

Mr. Smith: I **will go** on a vacation next week.

NOW

Present Tense and Present Continuous

Principal Parts 1 and 3 are both used to express something that happens at the present time. The explanations below point out when each is used.

The simple present tense form of any verb is identical to Principal Part 1 , the base form of the verb, except that **-s** or **-es** is added to the base form of third-person singular forms.

Action in the present can be expressed in two ways—as the simple present with one verb (see below, left side) and as the present continuous with two verbs (see below, right side).

1 Present Tense

I eat breakfast every day.

eat

Base Form

Today:
Habits and
Repetitive Actions

3 **Present Continuous**

I am eating breakfast now.

am eating

Helping Verb   *Present Participle*

Today:
Actions in Progress
and Continuous Actions

| Andy states: **I eat breakfast every day.** It is a *habit, a repetition that happens daily.* Use the base form of the verb, in this case, **eat**. | Andy says: **I am eating breakfast now**, so we assume he is *in the process* of eating. It is a *continuous action*. Use **am, are,** or **is** before the present participle of the verb, in this, case, **eating**. |

The *present continuous* states an action or condition that is taking place at the present moment.

YESTERDAY

Past Tense and Present Perfect

Principal Parts 2 and 4 are both used to relate events to the past, but they express time in different ways.

The *past tense* of a verb expresses an action or condition that took place in the past.

2 Past Tense   ## 4 Present Perfect

> I ate fish yesterday.

> I have eaten fish many times.

ate

Past Tense

Specific time in the past

have eaten

Helping Verb   Past Participle

Nonspecific completed actions

In the sentence **I ate fish yesterday**, the action did not take place today, but happened yesterday. The verb form **ate** indicates the past tense of the irregular verb **to eat.** It is a completed action that is now over. In addition, the word **yesterday** gives a *specific time* for when it happened.

In the sentence **I have eaten fish many times**, the present perfect refers to an action begun in the past but connected to the present; it may have been completed or it may still be going on. It is formed by using **have** together with the past participle, in this case, **eaten.**

Present perfect **verb forms show action or condition begun in the past; these can be either finished actions or actions that continue into the present.**

In the sentence **I have started piano lessons**, the verb form **started** is the past participle. It is assumed that Andy's lessons began in the past and continue into the present.

TOMORROW

Future Tense

The future tense uses "will" or "shall" and the base form of a verb.

	Subject Pronoun	Helping Verb	Base Form	Subject Pronoun	Helping Verb	Base Form
Future Tense	① I	will		① I	will	
	② you	will		② you	will	
	③ he, she, it (or Singular Noun)	will	walk	③ he, she, it (or Singular Noun)	will	write
	① we	will		① we	will	
	② you	will		② you	will	
	③ they (or Plural Noun)	will		③ they (or Plural Noun)	will	

The simple future (using "will") and the immediate future (using "going to ...") both indicate that an action or condition will happen in the future.

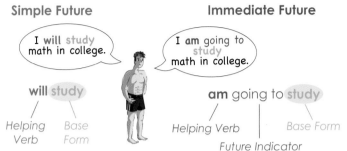

Simple Future

I will study math in college.

will study

Helping Verb / Base Form

Tomorrow: Actions that will happen in the future

Immediate Future

I am going to study math in college.

am going to study

Helping Verb / Future Indicator / Base Form

Tomorrow: Actions that are planned to happen in the future

The future tense of any verb is formed by using **will** with the base form of a verb. **Will** is used to connect to all subjects and shows no change.

Another way to express future time is by using forms of the verb **to be** (such as **am**, **are**, or **is**) with **going to** plus the base form of a verb. Always use the form **going to** as a Future Indicator; it does not change.

Simple Future

I **will** participate in the swim meet tomorrow.

Helping Verb / Base Form

Immediate Future

I **am** going to participate in the swim meet tomorrow.

Helping Verb / Future Indicator / Base Form

Look at the example **I am going to participate in the swim meet tomorrow**. The verb form **am** connects to the subject **I**. **Going to** indicates future action and never changes in form. **Participate** is the base form of the verb and is added after **going to**.

This concludes the section on tenses. Next, we continue to build on your knowledge of helping verbs, but add new details on how they are used.

4.11 Special Helping Verbs: Modals

The pattern of using a helping verb with the base form of a verb also applies to another kind of helping verb: *modals*. Modals are used to predict an action or condition, or to make a statement that is not a simple fact. Some common modals are **can**, **could**, **may**, **might**, **must**, **should**, and **would**.

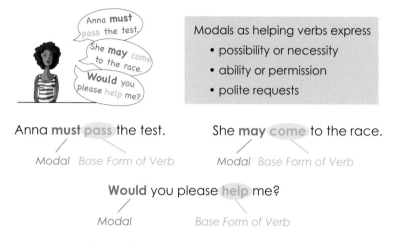

Modals as helping verbs express

- possibility or necessity
- ability or permission
- polite requests

Anna **must** pass the test.
Modal   Base Form of Verb

She **may** come to the race.
Modal   Base Form of Verb

Would you please help me?
Modal   Base Form of Verb

As helping verbs, modals connect to the base form of a verb. **Pass**, **come**, and **help** are the base forms used in the examples. They are main verbs; the modals help them to express meaning.

You will learn many other modals. Apply the same concept when using them.

> *Modals* **never change in form.**
> **They connect to the base form of a verb.**

4.12 Linking Verb *To Be* as Main Verb

When looking at the definitions of verb tenses, the terms *action* and *condition* appear often. *Action verbs* like **eat**, **swim**, and **go** refer to an action that takes place. *Linking verbs,* on the other hand, show no action or physical event occurring. They indicate conditions showing what the subject is, or is like.

The most common linking verb is **to be**. It shows being and existing. When learning about tenses, you used the helping verb **to be** together with a main verb. **To be** also performs another job: It can be used as a main verb, just like other verbs. But first, you must learn about all the different forms that the verb **to be** can take when it is used as a main verb.

Following are commonly used verb forms of the linking verb **to be**. Note that the verb is irregular in most forms.

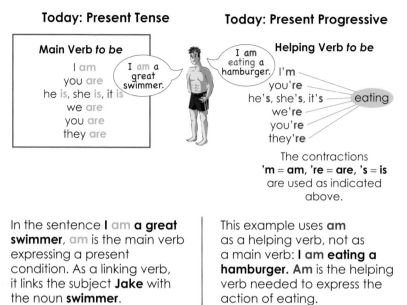

Today: Present Tense

Main Verb *to be*

I am
you are
he is, she is, it is
we are
you are
they are

I am a great swimmer.

Today: Present Progressive

I am eating a hamburger.

Helping Verb *to be*

I'm
you're
he's, she's, it's
we're
you're
they're

eating

The contractions
'm = am, 're = are, 's = is
are used as indicated above.

In the sentence **I am a great swimmer**, am is the main verb expressing a present condition. As a linking verb, it links the subject **Jake** with the noun **swimmer**.

This example uses **am** as a helping verb, not as a main verb: **I am eating a hamburger**. **Am** is the helping verb needed to express the action of eating.

> **In the present tense, "am," "are," and "is" are the verb forms of the linking verb "to be" used as a main verb.**

Use the base form of **be** as the main verb when expressing the future.

Tomorrow: Future Tense

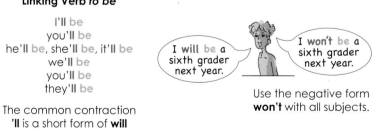

Linking Verb *to be*

I'll be
you'll be
he'll be, she'll be, it'll be
we'll be
you'll be
they'll be

The common contraction **'ll** is a short form of **will** and is used with all subjects.

I will be a sixth grader next year.

I won't be a sixth grader next year.

Use the negative form **won't** with all subjects.

Be is the main verb in the sentence **I will *be* a sixth grader next year**. Together with the helping verb **will**, it expresses a condition that will happen in the future.

In the past tense, "was" and "were" represent the verb forms of the linking verb "to be" used as a main verb.

Main Verb *to be*

I was
you were
he was, she was, it was
we were
you were
they were

In the first example, **hungry** describes the subject **Jake**. The second example uses **hungry** again to describe the subject **we**. **Last night**, a time indicator, refers to a past action as expressed by the verbs **was** and **were**.

4.13 Non-Action Verb *To Have* as Main Verb

The helping verb **to have** can also act as a main verb. When used alone, it names what the subject owns or holds.

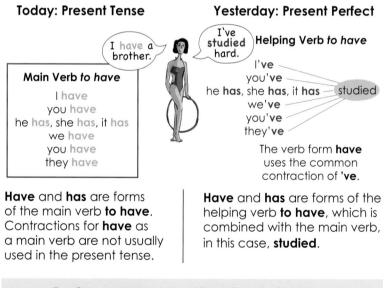

Today: Present Tense

Main Verb *to have*

I have
you have
he has, she has, it has
we have
you have
they have

Yesterday: Present Perfect

Helping Verb *to have*

I've
you've
he has, she has, it has — studied
we've
you've
they've

The verb form **have** uses the common contraction of **'ve**.

Have and **has** are forms of the main verb **to have**. Contractions for **have** as a main verb are not usually used in the present tense.

Have and **has** are forms of the helping verb **to have**, which is combined with the main verb, in this case, **studied**.

In the present tense, "have" and "has" are the main verb forms of "to have."

The past tense form of "to have" as a main verb is "had."

Main Verb *to have*
I had
you had
he had, she had, it had
we had
you had
they had

Ben **had** a pet.

The verb form **had** is used with all subjects. The name **Ben** is the subject of the example sentence above. The form **had** indicates that he no longer owns a pet. It indicates a past event: The action of owning a dog has ended.

4.14 Main and Helping Verbs in Questions and Statements

Questions

There are two main kinds of questions in English:

Questions beginning with a main or helping verb
Questions beginning with a question marker

For both kinds of questions, you will need to learn about word order in statements and questions.

Questions Beginning with a Main or Helping Verb

The following illustration shows the subject-position change that often occurs in questions.

Regular Word Order	**Inverted Word Order**
Subject Verb	Helping Verb Subject Main Verb
OR	OR
Subject Helping Main Verb Verb	Main Verb Subject

The Subject in the first position represents regular word order. With inverted word order, the main or helping verb comes *before* the Subject, which follows it in the second position.

A form of "to do," in either present or past tense, must be used to form questions, unless the main verb is the linking verb "to be."

The following charts illustrate word order using the helping verb **to do** in emphatic statements and direct questions, in both the present and past tenses.

Word Order in the Present Tense

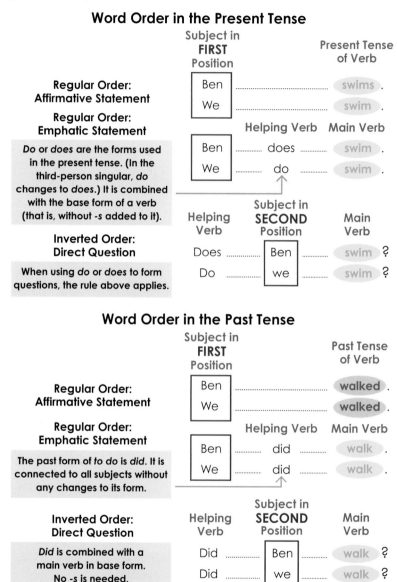

	Subject in **FIRST** Position		Present Tense of Verb
Regular Order: Affirmative Statement	Ben		swims .
	We		swim .
Regular Order: Emphatic Statement		Helping Verb	Main Verb
Do or does are the forms used in the present tense. (In the third-person singular, do changes to does.) It is combined with the base form of a verb (that is, without -s added to it).	Ben	does	swim .
	We	do	swim .
	Helping Verb	Subject in **SECOND** Position	Main Verb
Inverted Order: Direct Question	Does	Ben	swim ?
When using do or does to form questions, the rule above applies.	Do	we	swim ?

Word Order in the Past Tense

	Subject in **FIRST** Position		Past Tense of Verb
Regular Order: Affirmative Statement	Ben		walked .
	We		walked .
Regular Order: Emphatic Statement		Helping Verb	Main Verb
The past form of *to do* is *did*. It is connected to all subjects without any changes to its form.	Ben	did	walk .
	We	did	walk .
	Helping Verb	Subject in **SECOND** Position	Main Verb
Inverted Order: Direct Question	Did	Ben	walk ?
Did is combined with a main verb in base form. No -s is needed.	Did	we	walk ?

> **When the helping verb "to do" is used to form questions, the helping verb connects the subject with the main verb that follows.**

84

The previous chart shows an affirmative statement formed in two ways. The most common way uses only a main verb. Occasionally, both **to do** and a main verb are used. When using **do** or **does**, you add emphasis to your statement. The first four examples in each section—all statements—illustrate the subject in the first position.

Questions that require only a "yes" or "no" answer are called *direct questions*. These are common in everyday language.

When forming direct questions, the subject **Ben** or **we** is placed after the helping verb **do** or **does**. Use the present tense form of **to do** (**do** or **does**) for present tense questions. Use the past tense form **did** for anything that happened yesterday. The last two examples in each section—all direct questions—illustrate the subject in the second position.

Look at the following examples showing how other main and helping verbs use the same pattern as the helping verb **to do**.

Examples: **What kind of verb starts the question?**

Is Jake in the pool? **Is**: main verb in present tense

Were you the winner? **Were**: main verb in past tense

Has he written a book? **Has**: helping verb + **written**: main verb past participle

Can we eat now? **Can**: helping verb + **eat**: main verb base form

Questions Beginning with a Question Marker

Like direct questions, most questions that begin with a question marker, such as **what**, **why**, **when**, and **how**, follow inverted word order. The question becomes an *information question* that needs a more detailed answer than "yes" or "no." The subject in an information question appears *after* the helping verb.

	Question Marker	Helping Verb	Subject	Main Verb
	What	did	the manager	fix ?
	Why	does	Maria	study ?
	When	do	we	eat ?

Inverted Order

Question Markers as Subjects

When a question begins with a question marker that *replaces* the subject, regular word order applies, because the question marker as subject is in the first position.

Who swims? Ben swims.

Question word asking for the subject.

What opens? The pool opens.

> **When "who" or "what" replaces the subject to form a question, regular word order applies.**

Use regular word order with verb phrases as well. For example: **Who** is swimming now? **Who** will swim next? (Refer to Chapter 3, Pronouns, to review the use of question words as subjects.)

When making negative statements in the present or past tense, use a form of **to do** and the word **not**.

Affirmative Statements Using *To Do* in Present Tense

My brother **does** eat hot dogs.

The pool **does** open today.

We **do** celebrate Halloween.

Negative Statements Using To Do in Present Tense

No, I **do not** eat hot dogs.

The pool **does not** open today.

We **do not** celebrate Halloween October 30th.

don't

doesn't

don't

Negative Statements Using To Do in Past Tense

No, I **did not** eat hot dogs yesterday.

The pool **did not** open last night.

We **did not** celebrate Halloween last year.

didn't

didn't

didn't

> **To form a negative statement,
> use "do," "does," or "did" and the word "not" together
> with the base form of the main verb.**

Note that negative statements in the present tense can use the contractions **don't** (**do not**) and **doesn't** (**does not**), and negative statements in the past tense can use the contraction **didn't** (**did not**).

4.15 Verbs with Direct Objects

Verbs have another important job to do: They can take objects. This chapter introduces direct objects only; objects of prepositions will be explained in the preposition chapter.

Action verbs can take direct objects. These verbs can express both physical action and non-physical action. Let's look first at verbs that express non-physical action. The following two examples use the verb **to love**.

Andy loves is a basic sentence with a subject and a verb.

Basic Sentence

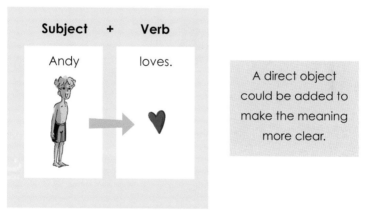

Subject + Verb

Andy   loves.

A direct object could be added to make the meaning more clear.

Many sentences require an additional word or group of words in order to be considered a complete thought. This word or group of words is called the *direct object* of the verb. Direct objects were introduced in Chapter 1. Now we show you how the action passes from a subject directly to the receiver.

Expanded Sentence

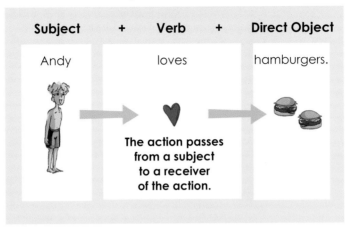

Subject	+	Verb	+	Direct Object
Andy		loves		hamburgers.

The action passes
from a subject
to a receiver
of the action.

In the example above, the noun **hamburgers** is the direct object. It receives the action expressed by the verb **loves**.

> **The *direct object* names the receiver of an action.
> It completes the meaning of the sentence.**

Direct objects are most commonly people, animals, places, or things. Here are two examples:

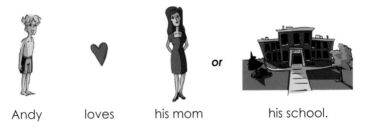

| Andy | loves | his mom | *or* | his school. |

A direct object is usually a noun or a pronoun. Please refer to Chapter 1, Nouns, and Chapter 3, Pronouns, to review explanations about direct objects.

4.16 Transitive and Intransitive Verbs

Verbs taking direct objects can also express physical action. Examples are fast-moving, energetic, action-packed verbs like **run**, **swim**, and **jump**.

A *transitive verb* has a direct object.

Expanded Sentence with a Direct Object

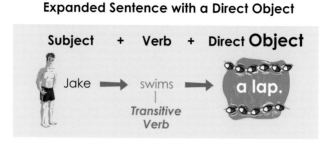

Subject + Verb + Direct **Object**

Jake → swims → a lap.

Transitive Verb

The direct object is the noun **a lap** that receives the action expressed by the verb **swims**. **Jake swims** is a basic sentence that can stand alone. If you add the direct object, a complete unit is formed by the subject, verb, and direct object, as indicated above. The verb **swims** takes the noun **a lap** as a direct object, and it is labeled as a transitive verb.

> ! *Hint: A verb is* **transitive** *when an object is necessary to complete its meaning in the sentence. The action of the verb is transferred to the object.*

Some verbs can be either transitive or intransitive, depending on the meaning of the sentence. The next example illustrates the verb **swims** as an intransitive verb.

An *intransitive verb* does not have a direct object.

Expanded Sentence with a Prepositional Phrase

Subject + Verb + Preposition + **Object** of Preposition

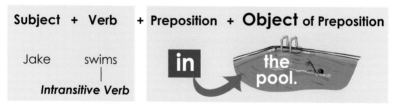

Jake   swims   **in**   the pool.

Intransitive Verb

Here, the verb **swims** does not have a direct object completing the sentence. Again, **Jake swims** is a basic sentence that can stand alone, but it can also be extended to include a prepositional phrase: **in the pool**. The noun **pool** is the object of the preposition **in**. In this sentence, the verb **swims** is an intransitive verb with no direct object. No action is transferred to an object in this sentence; the object of the preposition does not receive the action of the intransitive verb **swims**.

> **Hint:** *When an object is not needed to complete its meaning, the verb is* **intransitive**.

You will learn later why it is important to recognize transitive verbs. Learning about objects of prepositions is also important and is covered in Chapter 6, Prepositions.

4.17 Verbs Expressing Commands

**A sentence that gives a command
is called an *imperative sentence*.**

| A complete sentence can be just one word, like the command **Help!** | You often find these verbs on signs that give orders. What is the subject? It is **you**. The listener or reader knows that the word **you** is understood. |

Use imperative sentences to give commands or make requests, such as **Please pass the hamburgers** and **Go to the pool now**.

4.18 Overview of Verbs

Congratulations! The following charts summarize the *Four Principal Parts of a Verb*. Use these charts for a final review. Following the charts, you will find a list of 20 common irregular verbs and a Venn diagram that highlights the important concepts of helping verbs and main verbs.

Four Principal Parts of a Verb

Regular Verbs   Irregular Verbs

1 Base Form

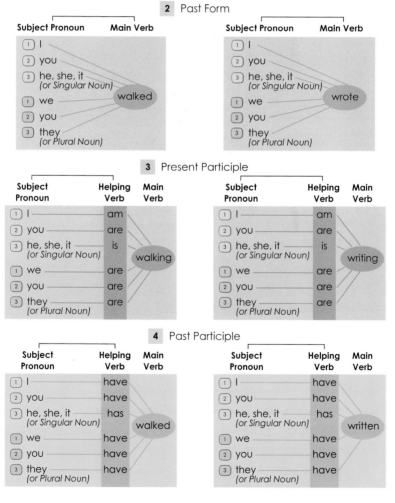

Note: The verb form used with third-person singular subjects shows a spelling change to the base form when it expresses an action in the present tense.

2 Past Form

3 Present Participle

4 Past Participle

Common Irregular Verbs

Verb Infinitive	1 Base Form of Verb	2 Past Form of Verb	3 Present Participle	4 Past Participle
1. to be*	be	was/were	being	been
2. to become	become	became	becoming	become
3. to bring	bring	brought	bringing	brought
4. to come	come	came	coming	come
5. to do*	do	did	doing	done
6. to drink	drink	drank	drinking	drunk
7. to drive	drive	drove	driving	driven
8. to eat	eat	ate	eating	eaten
9. to give	give	gave	giving	given
10. to go	go	went	going	gone
11. to have*	have	had	having	had
12. to know	know	knew	knowing	known
13. to leave	leave	left	leaving	left
14. to make	make	made	making	made
15. to see	see	saw	seeing	seen
16. to sleep	sleep	slept	sleeping	slept
17. to speak	speak	spoke	speaking	spoken
18. to swim	swim	swam	swimming	swum
19. to take	take	took	taking	taken
20. to write	write	wrote	writing	written

*Indicates a helping verb.

Main Verbs and Helping Verbs

Venn Diagram

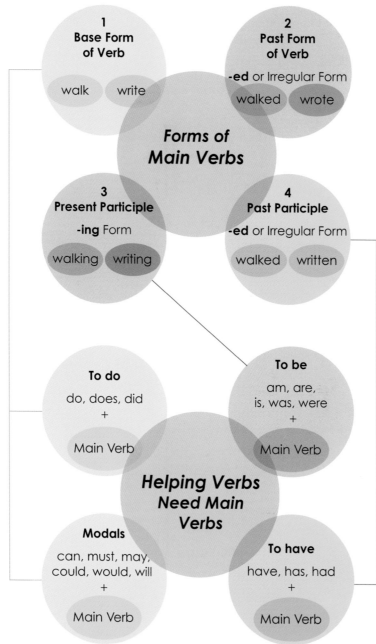

4.19 Review Exercises

A Fill in the blank with the correct form of the verb in parentheses. Use the present tense.

1. He _____ two brothers. (to have)
2. They _____ sixteen years old. (to be)
3. I _____ very tall. (to be)
4. Do we _____ dinner at 6:00 p.m.? (to eat)
5. The picture _____ blurry. (to be)

B Fill in the blank with the correct form of the verb in parentheses. Use the present continuous.

1. They _____ in the park. (to walk)
2. Anna _____ the package. (to send)
3. You _____ with a pen. (to write)
4. He _____ to music. (to listen)
5. I _____ a picture. (to draw)

C Fill in the blank with the correct form of the verb in parentheses. Use the past tense.

1. Jake _____ the box. (to open)
2. They _____ excited. (to be)
3. She _____ three laps. (to swim)
4. We _____ a goldfish. (to have)
5. You _____ three hot dogs! (to eat)

D Fill in the blank with the correct form of the verb in parentheses. Use the present perfect.

1. I _____ in New York. (to live)
2. Susan _____ the milk. (to spill)
3. They _____ their mother. (to call)
4. He _____ home. (to hurry)
5. We _____ the museum. (to visit)

E Fill in the blank with the correct form of the verb in parentheses. Use the future tense.

1. You _____ a steak. (to order)
2. She _____ famous. (to be)
3. I _____ my homework. (to do)
4. He _____ money. (to earn)
5. We _____ football. (to play)

F Underline the helping verb in the sentence. Circle the main verb.

1. He is typing.
2. We must study.
3. I have eaten.
4. You may enter the room.
5. They are singing.
6. She must dance.

G Write the past form of the verb.
Example: talk → talked

1. look   _____
2. march   _____
3. rub   _____
4. race   _____
5. warn   _____
6. try   _____

H There are three periods in time: present, past, and future. Determine whether the verb or verb phrase in red type illustrates an action in the present, past, or future. Write **present** if the action is in the present, **past** if it is in the past, or **future** if it is in the future.

1. He shall play the piano.   _____
2. She has lived here for a year. _____
3. I eat a sandwich for lunch.   _____
4. They won't sit on the bench.   _____
5. We wrote on the board.   _____
6. She is shopping.   _____

I Rewrite the statements below as questions by changing the word order and/or adding a form of "to do."
Examples: I am happy. → Am I happy?
             They like pizza. → Do they like pizza?

1. The dog is fast.   _____
2. He plays soccer well.   _____
3. We are at the theater.   _____
4. I have three sisters.   _____
5. She is writing a book.   _____
6. You have blue eyes.   _____

CHAPTER 5

ADVERBS

5.1 What Is an Adverb?

Adverbs act as modifiers. The prefix "ad-" in the word *adverb* means "to," "toward," or "in addition to." An adverb is a word that is used with a verb to expand its meaning.

walk
quietly

write
terribly

eat
slowly

swim
quickly

> ***Adverbs* add to or modify the meaning of verbs and are classified as adverbs of time, location, manner, degree, and frequency.**

Adverbs have many jobs to do. This section of the chapter introduces the main job adverbs perform: to modify verbs. Later in the chapter, we will cover how adverbs are used to modify both adverbs and adjectives.

5.2 Five Groups of Adverbs That Modify Verbs

Adverbs of Time

Adverbs of time tell when an action happened, happens, or will happen. Some of the most commonly used adverbs of time include **early**, **today**, **now**, **yesterday**, **before**, **soon**, and **tomorrow**.

When?

Halloween is coming **soon**.

Today tells you when the pool opens. Not just opens, but opens *today*.

Soon indicates when the holiday is coming. Not just coming, but coming *soon*.

Adverbs of Location

Adverbs of location tell where an action happened, happens, or will happen. Here are some examples of adverbs of location: **above**, **inside**, **here**, **there**, and **everywhere**.

Where?

Andy is walking **inside**.

Inside tells you where he
is walking. Not just walking,
but walking *inside*.

Here tells you where the
hot dogs are sold. Not just
sold, but sold *here*.

Adverbs of Manner

Adverbs of manner tell how something happened, happens,
or will happen. Some commonly used adverbs of manner are
loudly, **carefully**, **well**, **quickly**, and **slowly**.

How?

I eat **slowly**.

Walk **carefully** around the pool.

Carefully tells you how to walk.
Not just walk, but walk *carefully*.

Slowly tells you how he eats.
Not just eat, but eat *slowly*.

Adverbs of Degree

Adverbs of degree tell to what extent an action happened,
happens, or will happen. Here are some examples of this group
of adverbs: **completely**, **nearly**, **too**, **almost**, **very**, and **fully**.

I **nearly** hit the bottom of the pool!

To what extent?

I **almost** forgot my flippers!

Not just hit, but *nearly* hit.

Not just forgot, but *almost* forgot.

The examples above show the importance of understanding
adverbs: They tell you that the action did *not* happen in the end.

Adverbs of Frequency

Adverbs of frequency tell how frequently an action happened, happens, or will happen. Some commonly used adverbs of frequency are **always, often, sometimes, seldom,** and **never.**

How often?

Swimmers must **always** shower before entering the pool. Not just shower, but *always* shower.

The friends **often** walk to the pool. Not just walk, but *often* walk.

These five groups of adverbs are the most commonly used adverbs that modify verbs.

5.3 Adverbs Used to Form Questions

The question words that help you to identify the time, location, or manner of an action are called *interrogative adverbs.*

> **"When," "where," and "how" are used to form questions. They help you to identify the *time, location,* or *manner* of an action.**

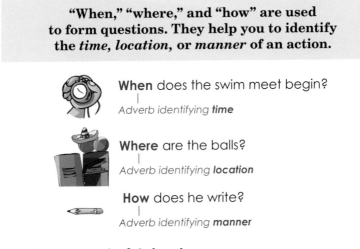

When does the swim meet begin?
|
*Adverb identifying **time***

Where are the balls?
|
*Adverb identifying **location***

How does he write?
|
*Adverb identifying **manner***

5.4 Placement of Adverbs

The placement of adverbs can vary greatly. Adverbs are usually placed directly *after* the verb. However, as the example **I almost forgot my flippers** shows, adverbs can also be placed *before* a verb. In the sentence **She walked around the pool carefully,** the adverb is placed after an object noun.

5.5 When Adjectives Become Adverbs

Most adjectives become adverbs by adding the suffix **-ly**.
This **-ly** suffix is a useful indicator to help you identify adverbs.

Adjectives
careless
bad
skillful
quick

Adverbs
carelessly
badly
skillfully
quickly

Even though the majority of adverbs are formed by adding **-ly**
to an adjective, not all adverbs have this suffix. Some examples
of adverbs that cannot be identified as adverbs by looking at
a suffix are **seldom**, **again**, **soon**, **almost**, **fast**, and **now**.

5.6 When Adverbs Modify Other Adverbs

**The meaning of an adverb can be made
stronger by adding a second adverb.**

In the examples below, the adverbs **very** and **really** are used
to modify other adverbs.

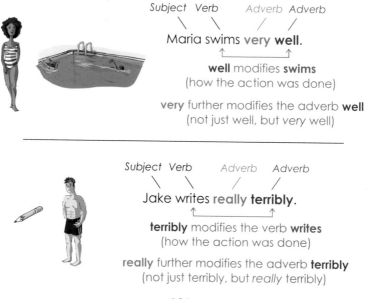

Subject   Verb   Adverb   Adverb

Maria swims **very well.**

well modifies **swims**
(how the action was done)

very further modifies the adverb **well**
(not just well, but *very* well)

Subject   Verb   Adverb   Adverb

Jake writes **really terribly.**

terribly modifies the verb **writes**
(how the action was done)

really further modifies the adverb **terribly**
(not just terribly, but *really* terribly)

101

5.7 When Adverbs Modify Adjectives

"Too" and "very" are commonly used adverbs of degree. They can modify adjectives as well as other adverbs.

Adverbs can be used to add more meaning to adjectives that describe a noun. Here is an example, expanded step by step.

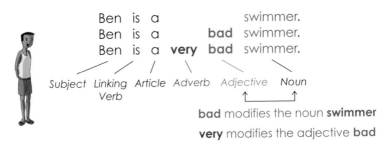

Ben is a swimmer.
Ben is a **bad** swimmer.
Ben is a **very bad** swimmer.

Subject Linking Article Adverb Adjective Noun
         Verb

bad modifies the noun **swimmer**

very modifies the adjective **bad**

In this example, the adverb **very** modifies the adjective **bad**. It explains to what extent Ben is a bad swimmer.

Adverbs of degree can modify both other adverbs and adjectives.

5.8 Comparison with Adverbs and Adjectives

The form of an adverb or adjective sometimes changes to show degrees of quality. In grammar, these changed forms showing a difference in degree constitute the *comparative form.*

There are three degrees of comparison in English:

1. The *positive degree* of an adjective or adverb describes a noun without comparing it to anyone or anything else. The positive degree of an adverb or adjective does not make a comparison.
2. The *comparative degree* shows that the quality as expressed by the adjective or adverb exists to a greater degree.
3. The *superlative degree* shows that the quality as expressed by the adjective or adverb exists to the greatest degree.

When adverbs or adjectives are used to compare, they change form or add new words to indicate degrees of quality.

The following chart shows two ways in which adjectives and adverbs form the comparative and superlative degrees. You can compare any person, place, thing, or idea to another one, or to a group of people, places, things, or ideas.

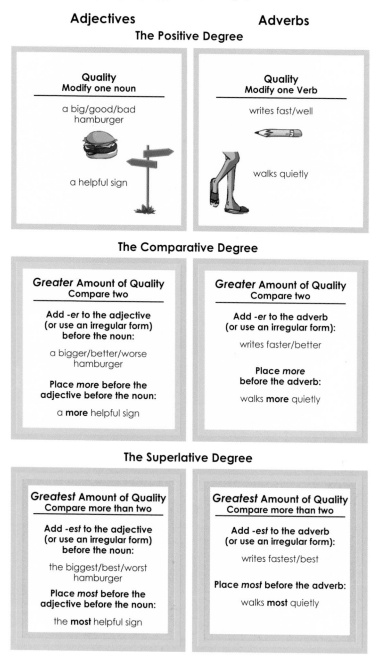

Adjectives   Adverbs

The Positive Degree

Quality
Modify one noun

a big/good/bad
hamburger

a helpful sign

Quality
Modify one Verb

writes fast/well

walks quietly

The Comparative Degree

***Greater* Amount of Quality**
Compare two

Add *-er* to the adjective
(or use an irregular form)
before the noun:

a bigger/better/worse
hamburger

Place *more* before the
adjective before the noun:

a **more** helpful sign

***Greater* Amount of Quality**
Compare two

Add *-er* to the adverb
(or use an irregular form):

writes faster/better

Place *more*
before the adverb:

walks **more** quietly

The Superlative Degree

***Greatest* Amount of Quality**
Compare more than two

Add *-est* to the adjective
(or use an irregular form)
before the noun:

the biggest/best/worst
hamburger

Place *most* before the
adjective before the noun:

the **most** helpful sign

***Greatest* Amount of Quality**
Compare more than two

Add *-est* to the adverb
(or use an irregular form):

writes fastest/best

Place *most* before the adverb:

walks **most** quietly

The previous chart includes adjectives and adverbs of comparison that have irregular forms. Irregular adjectives of comparison include **bad, worse, worst** and **good, better, best**. A common irregular adverb of comparison is **well, better, best**.

There are many other forms of adjectives and adverbs not mentioned in this summary. Make sure you continue to expand this list in order to use comparatives correctly.

5.9 Overview of Adjectives and Adverbs as Modifiers

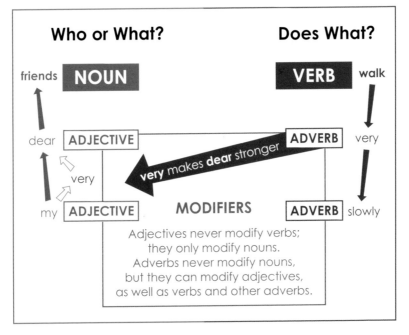

5.10 Review Exercises

A Identify the adverb in each sentence and underline it.

1. They swim slowly.
2. Mr. Miller cooks the meal well.
3. I almost fell down the stairs!
4. Dinner is nearly ready.
5. Anna really loves her family.
6. When is the test?
7. He eats breakfast early.
8. I read books quickly.
9. The sun shines brightly.
10. Do I write well?

B Determine whether the word in red type is an adverb or an adjective. Write **adv** if it is an adverb or **adj** if it is an adjective.

1. Shadow is a cute dog.   _____
2. She is very happy.   _____
3. We ask many questions.   _____
4. Ben really likes to surf!   _____
5. Where does he study?   _____
6. He talks more loudly.   _____
7. The directions are clear.   _____
8. Susan is swimming now.   _____

C Determine whether the adjective in red type is comparative or superlative. Write **C** for comparative or **S** for superlative.

1. I am the slowest runner.   _____
2. This pool is deeper than that pool. _____
3. His dog is smaller than my dog.   _____
4. She is the nicest girl in the school. _____
5. Jake is faster than Ryan.   _____
6. He is the most boring teacher!   _____
7. Maria is taller than Anna.   _____
8. Susan is the best swimmer.   _____

CHAPTER 6

PREPOSITIONS

Nouns Adjectives Pronouns Verbs Adverbs Prepositions Conjunctions Interjections

6.1 What Is a Preposition?

This chapter deals with another group of little words you need to understand: *prepositions*. Previous chapters showed how adverbs and adjectives add details to verbs and nouns. Prepositions are words that are placed before nouns or pronouns; they show a relationship in a sentence.

> A *preposition* is a word or group of words
> that is placed before a noun or a pronoun to show
> a relationship in a sentence.

In the illustration above, the phrases **inside the food cart**, **on top of the road**, and **at 9:00 a.m.** can be added to a basic sentence containing a subject and a verb, thus extending the sentence.

Example: Fred is **inside the food cart**.

The word **inside** is a preposition. It shows the relationship between Fred and the cart.

Example: The food cart sits **on top of the road**.

The words **on top of** function as a preposition and show the relationship between the food cart and the road.

Example: Fred's Foods opens today **at 9:00 a.m.**

The word **at** is a preposition and shows the relationship between Fred's Foods and 9:00 a.m.

As we explore the next section, you will see that each preposition shows a slightly different type of relationship.

6.2 What Prepositions Express

Here is an introduction to some of the prepositions in this chapter.

A closer look at these prepositions indicates that some prepositions express direction or movement. Other prepositions express location or time.

In this section, examples will help you learn how to distinguish between these three categories: *direction* or *movement, location,* and *time.* Note that the same preposition can be used in more than one category.

Direction or Movement

Example: Andy walks **into** the locker room.

Example: Andy walks **out of** the locker room.

The prepositions **into** and **out of** often express direction or movement of someone or something, usually from one place to another.

The question words **where** and **to where** can help you identify prepositions that express direction or movement.

Location

Joey sits **under** the umbrella.   The pep rally is **in** the school.

The preposition **in** often describes a location. Use **in** when the meaning is **within**. Place can refer to specific locations, such as *at your house,* or it can refer to a surface, such as *on top of the road.* The question word **where** can help you identify prepositions that express a location or a place.

Time

Pool Hours
9:00 a.m. –
10:00 p.m.

My birthday is **on** Easter.   The pool opens **at** 9:00 a.m.

The preposition **at** can be used to express both an event in time and time shown on a clock. The most common prepositions referring to time are **in**, **at**, and **on**. Other examples are *Graduation is in May* and *The party takes place on Saturday.* Use the question word **when** to identify prepositions that express time.

6.3 Frequently Used Prepositions

There are a great many prepositions. Only a few of the most common prepositions are shown in the list below.

——— Frequently Used Prepositions ———			
across	down	into	out
after	for	near	out of
at	from	of	over
before	in	off	to
behind	inside	on	with

6.4 Single-Word and Compound Prepositions

Prepositions can take the form of a single word. **At**, **in**, **out**, and **for** are some examples of *single-word prepositions*. Multiple-word prepositions are called *compound prepositions*. **Out of**, **in front of**, and **across from** are examples of prepositions that are composed of more than a single word.

6.5 Prepositional Phrases with Nouns and Pronouns

A *prepositional phrase* consists of two distinct parts. The first part is the preposition itself. The second part, which follows the preposition, is a noun or pronoun that is called the *object of the preposition*. Together, these two parts form what is called a *prepositional phrase*.

Prepositional Phrases with Nouns

Example:
Susan swims with Jake.

Preposition   Object (Noun)

with Jake = prepositional phrase

In this example, **with Jake** is a prepositional phrase. The preposition **with** is a single-word preposition. It is followed by the noun **Jake**. **Jake** is called the object of the preposition. A noun does not change in form when it becomes an object of a preposition.

> **A preposition and the object of the preposition form a *prepositional phrase*.**

Example:
The balls are on top of the locker.

Preposition   Object (Noun)

on top of the locker = prepositional phrase

The preposition **on top of** is a compound preposition composed of three words. The noun **locker** represents the object of the preposition. By combining the preposition **on top of** with the object noun **the locker**, you form a prepositional phrase.

Prepositional Phrases with Pronouns

Example:
Susan swims with him.

Preposition   Object (Pronoun)

with him = **prepositional phrase**

In this example, the preposition **with** is followed by the object pronoun **him**. A pronoun used as the object of a preposition must be an *object pronoun*; it cannot be a subject pronoun.

In the chart below, subject pronouns are listed on the left, and object pronouns are listed on the right. When you want to use a pronoun as the object of a preposition, you must choose it from the object pronouns in the chart on the right.

Subject Pronouns		Object Pronouns	
Singular	**Plural**	**Singular**	**Plural**
① I	① we	① me	① us
② you	② you	② you	② you
③ he, she, it	③ they	③ **him,** her, it	③ them

Using Object Pronouns

In order to form a correct prepositional phrase with a pronoun, you must be able to recognize and use object pronouns. To help you identify an object pronoun, try placing the preposition **with** before a pronoun to see if it makes sense. Using **with** before **he** does not make sense. You must select an object pronoun, in this case, the pronoun **him**. Any object pronoun listed on the chart above can be combined with a preposition.

6.6 Extended Units with Direct Objects and Objects of a Preposition

Direct objects and objects of a preposition are both used to expand the basic unit of a subject and a verb. Note, however, the differences in structure for the two examples that follow.

In the first example, the direct object is the noun **note**. It receives the action of the verb **write**. As an object, it is a building block and cannot stand alone. By adding **a note** to **Susan writes**, you expand the basic unit of subject and verb to include a direct object.

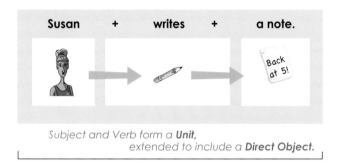

Subject and Verb form a **Unit**,
extended to include a **Direct Object**.

The sentence **Susan writes a note** is an extended unit.

The second example shows how a preposition combines with a noun to form a prepositional phrase. The preposition **under** and the noun **umbrella** form a prepositional phrase. This, too, is a building block that cannot stand alone.

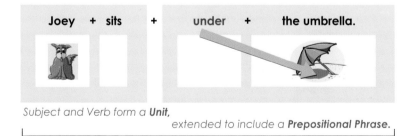

Subject and Verb form a **Unit**,
extended to include a **Prepositional Phrase**.

The prepositional phrase **under the umbrella** establishes a relationship between **Joey** (the subject) and **the umbrella** (the object of the preposition **under**).

Although **Joey sits** could stand alone as the smallest type of sentence, when you add **under the umbrella**, you extend

113

the basic unit of subject and verb to include a prepositional phrase. You have now formed an extended unit.

> **A prepositional phrase must have both a preposition *and* an object.**

Look for more examples of direct objects and prepositional phrases in this chapter as well as in Chapters 1, 2, and 3, so that you will be more familiar with these common ways to form extended units.

6.7 Some Words Are Both Prepositions and Adverbs

> **A preposition always has an object.**

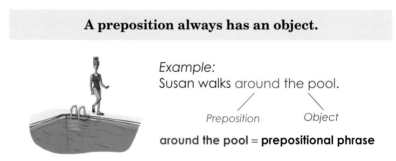

Example:
Susan walks around the pool.

Preposition   Object

around the pool = prepositional phrase

When you include **the pool** as the object of the preposition **around**, you have formed a proper prepositional phrase with both a preposition and an object.

However, some words can be used as prepositions when they have an object, but they can also be used as adverbs when they do not have an object.

Example: Susan walks around.

Adverb

This example illustrates when the word **around** cannot be called a preposition, because there is no object of a preposition. In this case, the word **around** is used as an *adverb* instead of as a preposition. You have already covered adverbs in Chapter 5.

> **An adverb never has an object.**

Look again at the phrases **walks around** and **around the pool** in the examples on the previous page. The following chart highlights the use of the word **around** as an adverb on the left and as a preposition on the right.

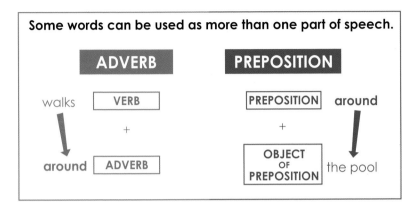

6.8 Review Exercises

A Underline the prepositions in the following sentences.

1. The book is on the shelf.
2. She gardens in the morning.
3. He does not walk to school.
4. Anna swims in the pool.
5. School starts at 8:00 a.m.
6. The ball goes in the net.
7. They sleep late on Saturdays.
8. She sits in the chair.
9. The plane flies over the ocean.

B Fill in the blank with the appropriate preposition. Refer to the list of frequently used prepositions in this chapter.

1. He runs _____ the street.
2. She sleeps _____ the bed.
3. He plays _____ his friends.
4. Dinner is _____ the table.
5. They eat lunch _____ 12:00 p.m.

C Determine whether the preposition in each sentence is a single-word or a compound preposition. Write **S** for a single-word preposition or **C** for a compound preposition.

1. The cat is on top of the chair. _____
2. Music plays on the radio. _____
3. Ben walks out of the room. _____
4. The sun sets at 7:00 p.m. _____
5. The car is in front of the house. _____
6. He drives on the road. _____
7. Susan buys gifts for her family. _____
8. Ryan sits across from Anna. _____
9. Her birthday is on Friday. _____
10. The dog eats off the floor. _____

CHAPTER 7

CONJUNCTIONS

7.1 What Is a Conjunction?

This is the final group of important words for forming sentences that we will study. The most common conjunctions that will be introduced in this chapter are **and**, **or**, and **but**.

> A *conjunction* **joins words or a group of words of the same type.**

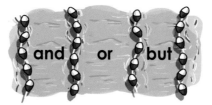

A *conjunction* is a word used to join similar elements in a sentence. These elements can be words, phrases, or sentences. The conjunctions introduced in this chapter are also called coordinating conjunctions, because they coordinate elements that are similar.

7.2 Joining Words

Here are examples that illustrate how conjunctions join words—first, nouns with nouns, and then, adjectives with adjectives.

• **and** expresses addition

The following example shows **and** used as a conjunction between two words.

Example: Anna **and** Jake

Noun   Conjunction   Noun

Two nouns—in this case, the names of people—are joined by the conjunction **and**, making it possible to form a sentence such as **Anna *and* Jake are friends**.

• **or** expresses a choice

The next example shows **or** used as a conjunction between two words.

Example: Maria **or** Anna

Noun   Conjunction   Noun

Two nouns are joined by the conjunction **or**, indicating a choice in a question such as **Can Maria *or* Anna come over?**

Conjunctions can be used to join adjectives as well.

Example: green **or** pink bikini

Adjective   Conjunction   Adjective

Two equal elements—adjectives—are joined by the conjunction **or**. A full sentence could read **Maria wears her green *or* pink bikini almost every day during the summer.**

7.3 Joining Phrases

In addition to joining two words of the same kind, conjunctions can also be used to join two phrases.

• **and** expresses addition

The following example shows **and** used as a conjunction between two prepositional phrases.

Example: For Jake **and** for Maria

Prepositional   Conjunction   Prepositional
Phrase   Phrase

Here, two prepositional phrases are joined by the conjunction **and**. A full sentence could read **The hula girl performed for Jake last week *and* for Maria this week.**

• **or** expresses a choice

The following example shows **or** used as a conjunction between two prepositional phrases.

Example:
Near the pool **or** in the locker room

Prepositional   Conjunction   Prepositional
Phrase   Phrase

Two prepositional phrases joined with the conjunction **or** could form the question **Is the lifesaver near the pool *or* in the locker room?**

7.4 Joining Sentences

Conjunctions can also combine two sentences, just as they join words or phrases.

• **and** expresses addition

The following example shows **and** used as a conjunction between two sentences.

We went to the pool.

The Miller family went to the parade.

We went to the pool, **and** the Miller family went to the parade.

Sentence   Conjunction   Sentence

In this example, two equal elements—in this case, two complete sentences—are joined by the conjunction **and**; they are now combined into a single sentence.

• **but** expresses contrast

The following example shows **but** used as a conjunction between two sentences.

All the friends came.
Maria was not there.

All the friends came, **but** Maria was not there.

Sentence   Conjunction   Sentence

The conjunction **but** is also used to combine two sentences into one. However, the use of the conjunction **but** expresses contrast in the sentence, while the conjunction **and** expresses addition.

Hint: When using conjunctions, make sure to join words or groups of words of the same type. Later in your studies, other conjunctions will be introduced that combine elements that are different. These conjunctions have different rules.

7.5 Review Exercises

A Underline the conjunction in each sentence.

1. Does Ben have a brother and a sister?
2. She plays the piano and the guitar.
3. Jake eats hot dogs or pizza for dinner.
4. Anna and Andy play outside.
5. The flowers are blue and pink.
6. He does not like eggs or bacon.
7. She sings and dances.

B Determine whether the conjunction in red type expresses addition, a choice, or contrast. Write **A** for addition, **CH** for a choice, or **C** for contrast.

1. Ben likes ice cream, but Susan likes popsicles. _____
2. She will go to the party or to the beach. _____
3. Maria and Jake watch television. _____
4. They see the stars and the moon. _____
5. The dog barks, but the cat purrs. _____
6. Ben walks or takes the bus. _____
7. He dives and jumps in the water. _____

C Complete each sentence with the appropriate conjunction. Choose one of the following: **and, or, but.**

1. He enjoys reading _____ running.
2. Will he dance with Susan _____ Maria?
3. Anna has brown hair _____ blue eyes.
4. He wants to swim, _____ she wants to surf.
5. Ben _____ Maria go to school together.
6. Does she like roses _____ tulips?
7. He likes football, _____ he prefers soccer.

CHAPTER 8

INTERJECTIONS

8.1 What Is an Interjection?

Interjections are sudden, interrupting words or phrases that are also known as *exclamations*. Common interjections include **wow**, **well**, **hey**, **bravo**, and **oh**.

> An *interjection* expresses strong emotion or surprise;
> it functions independently within a sentence.

Example: **Wow!** Look at that!

|
Interjection

In the example above, we see that the interjection **Wow!** stands apart from the rest of the sentence and adds an element of surprise.

> **Interjections are often signaled
> by an exclamation mark.**

Example: **Bravo!** You won the race!

|
Interjection

> **Interjections can also be signaled by a comma.**

Example: **Oh**, they are late.

|
Interjection

8.2 Review Exercises

A Determine whether each statement is true or false. Write **T** for true or **F** for false.

1. Interjections are never signaled by an exclamation mark. _____
2. An interjection functions independently within the sentence. _____
3. Interjections are also known as exclamations. _____
4. Interjections do not express strong emotion. _____
5. An interjection can be signaled by a comma. _____

B Fill in the blank with the appropriate interjection from the choices given.

1. _____, that dog is huge! (Wow | Bravo | Oh)
2. _____! We get to go to the beach! (Oh | Hooray | Well)
3. _____, can you hear me? (Hey | Bravo | Wow)
4. _____, I hope they can come. (Oh | Gosh | Uh-oh)

Congratulations!

Dear Student,

You have learned the basics of the English language, which is a major accomplishment. Now that you have been exposed to the fundamentals of English grammar, you have a strong foundation for future studies.

Don't forget that learning a language is an ongoing process. It doesn't end when you close this book. In fact, it is just beginning! We hope that this book has equipped you with tools that will help you as you progress in your studies. We wish you the best of luck as you expand your knowledge of the English language.

ANSWER KEY

1 NOUNS

A
1. Y   2. Y   3. N   4. Y   5. N   6. N   7. N   8. Y   9. N   10. Y

B
1. rings   2. leaves   3. beaches   4. clouds   5. berries   6. lives
7. birds   8. patches   9. nails   10. skies

C
1. a   2. an   3. a   4. a   5. an

D
1. He, (runs)   2. Anna, (swims)   3. father, (drives)
4. They, (sit)   5. cat, (jumps)

E
1. trees'   2. bike's   3. Chris'   4. building's   5. cars'

F
1. house, (big)   2. dog, (brown)   3. He, (short)   4. name, (Andy)
5. sky, (blue)

G
1. T   2. F   3. T   4. T   5. T

2 ADJECTIVES

A
1. loud   2. American   3. brown   4. small, full   5. orange
6. tired   7. cold   8. sad   9. colorful, beautiful

B
1. a, I   2. the, D   3. an, I   4. A, I   5. the, D

C
1. His   2. three   3. my   4. every   5. my   6. that   7. her

3 PRONOUNS

A
1. 3rd   2. 1st   3. 2nd   4. 1st   5. 3rd

B
1. S   2. P   3. P   4. S   5. S   6. P   7. P

C
1. P   2. X   3. X   4. P   5. P   6. X

D
1. SP   2. OP   3. OP   4. SP   5. OP   6. OP   7. SP

E
1. It   2. whom   3. ours   4. I   5. Those   6. her

4 VERBS

A
1. has   2. are   3. am   4. eat   5. is

B
1. are walking   2. is sending   3. are writing   4. is listening
5. am drawing

C
1. opened   2. were   3. swam   4. had   5. ate

D
1. have lived   2. has spilled   3. have called   4. has hurried
5. have visited

E
1. will order   2. will be   3. will do   4. will earn   5. will play

F
1. is (typing)   2. must (study)   3. have (eaten)   4. may (enter)
5. are (singing)   6. must (dance)

G
1. looked   2. marched   3. rubbed   4. raced   5. warned
6. tried

H
1. future   2. past   3. present   4. future   5. past   6. present

I
1. Is the dog fast?   2. Does he play soccer well?
3. Are we at the theater?   4. Do I have three sisters?
5. Is she writing a book?   6. Do you have blue eyes?

5 ADVERBS

A
1. slowly   2. well   3. almost   4. nearly   5. really   6. When
7. early   8. quickly   9. brightly   10. well

B
1. adj   2. adv   3. adj   4. adv   5. adv   6. adv   7. adj   8. adv

C
1. S   2. C   3. C   4. S   5. C   6. S   7. C   8. S

6 PREPOSITIONS

A
1. on   2. in   3. to   4. in   5. at   6. in   7. on   8. in   9. over

B
1. across   2. in   3. with   4. on   5. at

C
1. C   2. S   3. C   4. S   5. C   6. S   7. S   8. C   9. S   10. S

7 CONJUNCTIONS

A
1. and   2. and   3. or   4. and   5. and   6. or   7. and

B
1. C   2. CH   3. A   4. A   5. C   6. CH   7. A

C
1. and   2. or/and   3. and   4. but   5. and   6. or   7. but

8 INTERJECTIONS

A
1. F   2. T   3. T   4. F   5. T

B
1. Wow   2. Hooray   3. Hey   4. Gosh

About the Author

Gabriele Stobbe, a native of Düsseldorf, Germany, began her professional career as a kindergarten and art teacher. Having decided to pursue proficiency in foreign languages, she lived in France and Spain for several years. Travels with her husband took her to South America and South Africa, where she began her undergraduate career at the University of South Africa in Pretoria, completing it at Duquesne University in Pittsburgh, Pennsylvania.

After years of teaching languages in high schools and for the Bayer Corporation, she formed her own company to provide language services and private tutoring in German, French, and Spanish.

A move to Washington, D.C. brought her prestigious assignments at the Goethe Institute, the Foreign Service Institute for the Department of State, and the Johns Hopkins School for Advanced International Studies.

Gabriele's lifelong passion has been to provide effective learning materials that will assist students throughout the critical early stages of their language learning. You may visit her Web site at *elingopro.com*.